INVESTIGATI A

HOMICIDE

TIMOTHY SWEETMAN & ADELE SWEETMAN

WADSWORTH
CENGAGE Learning

Australia • Brazil • Japan • Korea • Mexico • Singapore • Spain • United Kingdom • United States

Investigating A Homicide
Timothy Sweetman & Adele Sweetman

For product information and technology assistance, contact us at
Cengage Learning Customer & Sales Support, 1-800-354-9706
For permission to use material from this text or product,
submit all requests online at **www.cengage.com/permissions**
Further permissions questions can be emailed to
permissionrequest@cengage.com

Library of Congress Control Number: 96-71590

ISBN-13: 978-0-942728-77-4

ISBN-10: 0-942728-77-7

Wadsworth
20 Davis Drive
Belmont, CA 94002-3098
USA

Cengage Learning is a leading provider of customized learning solutions with office locations around the globe, including Singapore, the United Kingdom, Australia, Mexico, Brazil, and Japan. Locate your local office at **www.cengage.com/global**

Cengage Learning products are represented in Canada by Nelson Education, Ltd.

To learn more about Wadsworth, visit **www.cengage.com/wadsworth**

Purchase any of our products at your local college store or at our preferred online store **www.cengagebrain.com**

Printed in the United States of America
14 15 16 17 18   22 21 20 19 18

Dedication

For Kathleen, Jack, Artie, Edmund, Lisa, and Sean, with love

Table of Contents

Chapter 4
The Autopsy 43

Chapter 5
Rochelle Moren 55

Chapter 6
Interrogation and Interview 67

Chapter 7
The Cellular Trail 81

Preface

Investigating a Homicide Workbook is designed to accommodate a semester of weekly in-class investigation. The following are suggestions—suggestions only, however, since we invite instructors to be as flexible and innovative as their classes allow.

First, to put students immediately in the investigative mindset, we suggest an informal, open reading. Ask each student to read a portion aloud. This allows instructors to clarify vocabulary, narrative and pronunciation.

Second, ask students to re-read the chapter themselves for individual understanding of the homicide and subsequent investigation before they answer the questions within each chapter. During this analytical process, students will need to look back and review the material to complete their detective work.

Third, ask students to pair up in groups to compare and discuss their individual findings, identity of suspect(s) and proof for an arrest and criminal filing.

Fourth, students in each group must consider and challenge each other's input with a critical mind and detective reasoning. A moderator should be selected to keep each student involved, log the groups' agreed upon investigative findings and opinions and report on them.

Fifth, class discussion follows.

Sixth, students should submit their individual worksheets to the instructor for review and to receive credit for participating in the investigation.

Timothy Sweetman
Adele Sweetman

About the Authors

Tim Sweetman spent 13 years in law enforcement. He worked Patrol, Community Relations, Street Gang and Narcotics before spending three years as a homicide detective and a year as a homicide sergeant. Currently, he is a full-time Administration of Justice instructor at Los Angeles City College, Los Angeles, California. He earned a Master of Arts degree in Public Administration at California State University, Northridge, a Bachelor of Science degree in Marketing from California State Polytechnic University, Pomona and an Associate of Arts degree in Administration of Justice at Pasadena City College.

Adele Sweetman writes True-Crime. She is also an English professor at DeVry Institute of Technology and Rio Hondo College in Los Angeles County, California. She earned her Master of Arts degree in Creative Writing at California State University, Northridge, a Bachelor of Arts degree in English at California Polytechnic University, Pomona and an American Bar Association Certified Litigation Legal Assistant Specialist degree at California State University, Los Angeles.

Declaration

The persons portrayed in this text are actual people—some living, some dead. However, to protect their privacy, the names of these individuals have been changed.

Chapter 1

There's Been a Homicide

On Friday, April 27, you closed out your investigation on a major case that happened two weeks ago. On Monday, you will have a good case to present to the district attorney for a criminal filing. You stayed in the office until after midnight to finish all the paperwork; you returned home Saturday morning at about 1:00 a.m., turned off your alarm clock—which wakes you at 6:30 a.m. during the week—and quickly fell asleep.

April 28 (Saturday)

At 6:00 a.m. you are awakened by the telephone; it's Sergeant Sandoval. "Detective, I'm sorry to wake you, but we've had a homicide."

You're groggy, but instinctively ask for details.

"All I know is that a newspaperman found a lady in the middle of a street, the sergeant says. She was shot in the head. We think she was a prostitute."

"What makes you think that?"

"The way she's dressed."

"Okay."

"Do you want me to call the coroner?" The patrol sergeant asks.

"No. I'll need to see the scene first. I'll be in the office in about an hour."

"Okay, see you then."

An hour later you are at the station; your partner had been called and is there as well.

"What's the latest?" You ask Sergeant Sandoval.

"Nothing more. The officers have sealed off the area and are waiting for you."

You and your partner drive to Mountain Avenue and Page Place, park away from the scene and walk to the area sealed off by yellow police tape. Two officers and an evidence technician are standing by.

Officers' Statements

The officers brief you and your partner about whom they have interviewed and what they have seen and done. They tell you they arrived at 5:30 a.m. and met the newspaperman at the corner of Mountain Avenue and Page Place. He directed them to the body of a female whose face was lying in a pool of blood.

The officers explain that the victim appeared to have sustained a bullet wound to the right side of her head. They say when they arrived, she was lying on her stomach in a northerly direction, her head turned, facing east and her wound exposed. Her legs were fully extended; her arms were extended underneath her body. They added that the woman was clothed in a blue evening dress. In addition, the woman's purse was lying on the ground between her feet. The officers have speculated that the victim may have been a prostitute because her dress is typical of that profession and her makeup is on the heavy side.

The officers tell you that, upon further review of the scene, they saw two music cassettes near the woman's feet, a pack of Kool cigarettes on the street approximately eight feet from the victim's body, and two spent bullet casings near the victim— one approximately a foot away from the woman's head and the other approximately two and a half feet from the center of the body. There was also a bullet projectile on the ground by the victim's left shoe.

The officers add that shortly after their arrival, the paramedics arrived and administered some type of medical treatment to the woman. The paramedics turned the woman on her back, sheared her dress down the center and attempted to revive her, but they were unable to do so. They pronounced the victim dead at 5:38 a.m.

The officers secured the perimeter of the scene; they placed yellow police tape across the street, two houses to the east and two houses to the west of the body.

The officers stated that two other police officers arrived at the scene and helped locate possible witnesses. The physical evidence technician arrived and began photographing and sketching the crime scene.

Witnesses

You have the officers brief you as to witnesses' statements prior to you and your partner inspecting the crime scene in order to give you as much information as possible in helping to recover evidence.

Witnesses, especially eyewitnesses, can provide information as to who committed the crime and how; this will help you locate evidence at the crime scene and elsewhere. Also, if a suspect is known, you must arrange to locate or surveil the suspect immediately. In addition, you will want to identify and conduct a more in-depth interview with witnesses who will help your investigation. You often request that witnesses remain available so you can conduct interviews after you inspect the crime scene.

Mr. Jones, a newspaper delivery man, told the officers that at about *5:20 a.m. he was delivering his newspapers on Mountain Avenue, in the City of Pasadena, when he saw a body lying on the street. Mr. Jones said that the body was motionless, but he could not see bodily injury. Nevertheless, he drove to a pay phone on Page Place and called the police. During this time, he said he saw a white Volkswagen Bug driving down Page Place. The car was occupied by two males. The driver turned west on Mountain Avenue and immediately turned around and headed back onto Page Place. It occurred to him that the occupants in the car probably saw the body. Mr. Jones waited by the telephone until the police arrived.

Mr. Duran stated he was awakened by a car horn at approximately *5:15 a.m. He said he walked out of his residence, on Mountain Avenue, to see if anything was wrong and saw the female lying on her stomach. She was bleeding heavily from the face. Mr. Duran said he got about five feet from the body before he went back into his house and called the police. Mr. Duran could not add anything further.

Mr. Wellman was working at a power plant, a block away, and heard what sounded like two gunshots at about *4:30 a.m. Shortly after, he saw a small dark car drive eastbound on Mountain Avenue, then southbound on Page Place toward the freeway. Mr. Wellman said that this occurred about 20 seconds after the shots. He told the officers he didn't think much of the situation until he saw the police arrive, so he walked to the scene and contacted the officers.

Mrs. Taylor related that she and her husband were awakened by what sounded like gunshots and noticed it was *4:20 a.m. She added that neither she nor her husband heard arguing or the sound of a car.

Ms. Walker stated that she was awakened about *4:20 a.m. by a loud noise, but, since her dog did not bark, she went back to sleep.

Mr. Hamilton answered the officer's knock on the door but said he did not see or hear anything during the night.

The officers also knocked at 3780 Mountain Avenue, 3790 Mountain Avenue and 3820 Mountain Avenue but got no answer.

*Times are not always accurate as related by the witnesses. Detectives need to be cognizant of this and not rely on the exact time unless it is specifically documented by a reliable source, e.g. computer or a time stamp. Witnesses can be off by minutes or even hours depending on the situation.

Officer Walk-Through

An officer takes you and your partner on a walk-through of the crime scene. She shows you where the body was positioned before the paramedics rolled the body over. She points out the two shell casings and the spent bullet. The officer also shows you the purse, music tapes and cigarette package.

Crime Scene Inspection

Evidence markings: Before evidence technicians sketch, photograph and retrieve evidence from the crime scene, they mark the items to be retrieved with numbered placards. This identifies evidence in the photographs and the sketch and also organizes the collection and documentation of the evidence items.

You and your partner take a close look at the victim's head. You see that she was shot at least two times. You determine, from the size of the holes, that the bullets were of small caliber. In addition, you believe that one shot entered her right temple and one entered near her left cheek. There appears to be an exit wound just above the left cheek. You scan the rest of her body and you see a puncture wound to her left forearm.

How did she get these wounds? You and your partner pose this question. You direct the evidence technician to take close-up photographs of the wounds. You also have the photographer take a photograph of a diamond ring on her left ring finger.

In addition, you look at her clothing and notice she is wearing a girdle. You question the prostitution theory because prostitutes don't generally wear girdles.

You take the purse and carefully inspect its contents; it is merely a makeup bag. It contains a lipstick, powder compact and small mirror. You notice that several feet beyond the purse is a pack of open *Zig-Zag* rolling papers. In addition, you notice a white hand towel (like those typically found in hotel rooms) lying on a patch of dirt off the south side of the road.

After the evidence technician marks and photographs the casings, bullet, cassette tapes, packs of cigarettes, *Zig-Zag* papers and white hand towel, you and your partner take a closer look at the evidence. The casings are .25 caliber, the bullet also appears small in caliber and consistent with .25 caliber. One cassette tape is marked "Enchantment," the other "Guy." The cigarette package is open and mostly full. The *Zig-Zag* package is full. The towel is clean. You direct the photographer to take close-ups of all of this evidence.

You and your partner now conduct a close inspection of the crime scene and find the following items:

1. Two miniature bottles of vodka are lying several yards west of the body on the north side of the road.

2. Tire tracks are in a dirt area on the south side of the road leading east.

3. A partial tennis shoe print is in the dirt by the tire tracks.

You direct the photographer to take close-up photographs of this evidence. You make sure that the photographer gets pictures of the tread marks left by the tires and the pattern of the shoe. You note the tire width and deduce that the tread marks were left by a small car.

PC 187

REFERENCE TO:

	Date of this report	Case number

N

GARAGE

15FT VOGUE

3FT VOGUE

18FT

5FT

4FT

VICTIM

BLOOD

HORIZON

ROAD

381 FT

95FT

7FT

178FT

263FT

26FT

24FT

17FT

8FT

6FT 2W

TIREMARKS

PAGE PLACE

MOUNTAIN AVENUE

LEGEND
1. BULLET CASINGS
2. BULLET CASTINGS
3. BULLET PROJECTILE
4. PKG OF KOOL CIGARETTES
5. AUDIO TAPE (ENCHANTMENTS GREATEST HITS)
6. AUDIO TAPE (GUY)
7. WHITE TOWEL
8. ZIG ZAG CIGARETTE PAPERS

Copies to	Copies Made By	Approved	Officer — P. No.

You call the coroner's office; the representative tells you the coroner investigator and the assistant will be there within an hour. During this time, your partner stays at the scene and assists the evidence technician in measuring the scene and collecting the evidence.

You walk to 3780 Mountain Avenue and contact resident, Ms. Dominguez. She tells you that about 4:25 a.m. she was awakened by loud noises and by the sound of screeching tires coming from down the street. She says she looked out the window and saw a small black car driving east toward Page Place. This witness did not see the occupant(s) in the car and couldn't describe it very well because she was sleepy; she adds, however, that the car's lights were off as it drove away. The resident further states that she didn't see anyone on the street because it was too dark—there are no street lights on Mountain Avenue.

You knock on the doors of the other two residents the officers, earlier, attempted to question. You don't get an answer; you leave a business card on the door requesting that they call you.

Next stop is an all-night gas station at the corner of Glen Street and Page Place. The attendant, a very tired Mr. Guzel, tells you he didn't see a car leave the crime scene area, he didn't service anyone who matched the victim's description and he didn't service a small dark car, period. You believe him. You see the coroner investigator arrive, and you walk back to the crime scene.

Coroner Investigator

Gunshot Residue (GSR): When a handgun is fired it emits barium and antimony powder. Residue will usually affix to the outer webbing of the hand holding the weapon. During a GSR test a chemical is sprayed onto the hands of a suspected shooter, then swabbed with Q-tips. Q-tips are analyzed for the barium and antimony. Gunshot residue can be found on skin, clothing or gloves; chances of detecting residue are reduced over time, after eight hours they are generally eliminated. Cleansed hands or clothing will also reduce or eliminate the chances of finding GSR.

Entrance Wounds: Entrance wounds typically indent the skin and are slightly larger or smaller than the size of the bullet. At close range, bullet holes will be slightly larger because of the explosive gases. At longer distances, 18" or more, the gases dissipate into the atmosphere so wounds are slightly smaller. In addition, entrance wounds leave a gray ring around the wound because, as the bullet passes through the skin, residue is deposited onto the skin.

Exit Wounds: Exit wounds are usually larger and bleed more than entry wounds. They are also usually shaped irregular because bullets often get fragmented when they travel through a body and push matter ahead of it.

Fingernail Scrapings: A coroner investigator gathers fingernail scrapings from death victims to obtain trace evidence such as blood, fibers, hair, etc. left, possibly, by the suspect.

It's about 8:30 a.m. when the coroner investigator arrives with her assistant. She issues you a coroner's case number and a Gunshot Residue number (GSR). You watch as the investigator feels the victim's face and head for additional wounds; she tells you it looks like the victim was shot three times—one entry wound to the right temple with an exit wound to the left cheek, one entry wound to the left cheek below the exit wound and another entry wound near the back of the left ear.

The investigator takes the victim's temperature with a thermometer by puncturing the skin and placing the thermometer in the liver; it reads 92 degrees. (The rule is that body temperature drops one and a half degrees every hour after death for the first six hours, and then one degree per hour thereafter depending on a variety of factors: outside temperature, type of clothing, size of the victim, body fat, etc.) At 8:55 a.m. the outside temperature is 76 degrees.

The coroner investigator takes fingernail scrapings and a hair sample from the victim. She swabs the victim's hands to test for gunshot residue. You request that a sexual assault examination be conducted by a criminalist. The investigator acknowledges your request but is more intent on the markings on the victim's left arm; she says they resemble intravenous track marks, indicative of I.V. drug abuse.

Coroner Investigator's Findings

Defense Wounds: Wounds that victims receive protecting themselves, usually associated with stab wounds. Typically, these wounds are seen on palms and forearms.

Postmortem Lividity: Upon death, blood settles and clots in the tissues. This causes a dark discoloration under the skin of those body parts nearest to the ground but not touching the ground. Coloring can begin soon after death; it can be pronounced several hours later. Due to clotting, even if the body is moved or repositioned, the discoloration remains in its original position.

Rigor Mortis: Upon death, the body muscles stiffen due to chemical changes in the muscle tissues. Rigor mortis varies depending on environmental conditions though, generally, the smaller muscles begin to stiffen 2 to 4 hours after death and extends to the larger muscles within 6 to 12 hours. Both muscle groups relax within 36 hours. (If the body is bent over or arms are extended upon death, it will remain is this stiffened position when it is lifted.)

The investigator does not observe lividity and notes only slight rigor mortis. She also checks for defense wounds on the hands and abrasions to the knees but finds none.

The coroner investigator and assistant wrap the body in plastic, place it on a gurney and push it into a van. You sign an inventory log that details the victim's only property:

1. A white stone ring

You request that the coroner's office notify you prior to the autopsy which will be in two or three days.

Name(s) _____   Date ____/____/____

_____

QUESTIONS - CHAPTER 1

1. Why did you advise the sergeant to wait before notifying the coroner's office?

2. What was the most important part of the officers' statements?

3. What information from the witnesses' statements is consistent?

4. What, if any, was the significance of a car driven at night with its lights off? Explain.

Name(s) _____   Date ____/____/____

_____

QUESTIONS - CHAPTER 1 CONTINUED

5. Did you find any potential evidence that the officers missed? Name the items.

6. What did you learn about the wounds sustained by the victim, and her clothing and jewelry, during the crime scene inspection?

7. What did you learn from the coroner investigator's inspection of the body?

Name(s) _____   Date _____/_____/_____

_____

QUESTIONS - CHAPTER 1 CONTINUED

8. Why did the coroner investigator do the following things:

    Take a gunshot residue (GSR) swab?

    Take a temperature reading?

    Conduct a physical/clothing inspection?

9. What does "no lividity" mean?

Name(s) _____   Date _____/_____/_____

_____

QUESTIONS - CHAPTER 1 CONTINUED

10. What does "slight rigor mortis" mean?

11. Why did you ask for a sexual assault examination?

12. What made you think the victim was not a prostitute?

13. What do you think may have happened from what you learned so far?

Chapter 2

The Mercury Hotel

April 28 (Saturday) *continued*

At 11:00 a.m. you and your partner are notified that a purse was found by a security officer in the parking lot of the Mercury Hotel. The officer who contacted you by radio says that the contents of the purse were scattered, but that he found identification.

"You may want to come by," the officer says.

You and your partner drive to the hotel. You look at the leather purse and its contents, and you find a driver's license that matches the identity of the murder victim; Cheryl Claymore was 26-years-old. There is also an address book.

Names _____   Date _____/____/____

_____

QUESTION - CHAPTER TWO

1. What do you do at this point?

   A. Return to the police station and look through the address book? Explain.

   B. Check N.C.I.C. to see if Cheryl was reported missing and follow-up at the hotel? Explain.

   C. Do nothing and hope the investigation will go away?

Interview With a Hotel Employee

You speak to a hotel employee and discover that Suei Lee, the desk clerk employee who checked Ms. Claymore into rooms 106 and 322, had already gone home. Nevertheless, you inquire about the rooms; you are relieved that neither room was subsequently rented and you immediately secure them as crime scenes.

Room 106, located on the ground level by the office, is clean with the exception of a pillow that is outside the bedding, lying lengthwise at the headboard. A black slip and a red bra are in a dresser drawer. You inspect room 322, on the third floor; the bedding is clean, pressed, undisturbed.

Names _____   Date ____/____/____

_____

QUESTIONS - CHAPTER 2 CONTINUED

2. Why is it important that neither room 106 nor 322 had been rented?

3. What potential pieces of evidence have you found, so far, in the rooms?

4. Is Cheryl's address book significant? Why?

5. What do you do next?

   A. Interview hotel personnel, such as the cleaning crew? Explain.

   B. Ignore the rooms because they've been cleaned? Explain.

   C. Wish that everything would go away?

Interview With the Cleaning Lady

In room 310 you find Shirley Townsend, the cleaning lady. She tells you, (your partner is with the evidence technician who has arrived and is going through room 106), that she cleaned room 322 and that the bed sheets are being laundered. She remembers that the sheets were messed-up and the comforter was partially hanging off the bed. Mrs. Townsend also tells you that there was a dry washcloth on the floor in the bathroom and a wet one hanging on the shower stall; both are being washed.

Mrs. Townsend also remembers that she found a cup on the nightstand next to the telephone and that it contained some type of liquid. She poured the liquid in the sink but, luckily, threw the cup into the litter bag attached to the cleaning cart.

You recover the cup and notice a small amount of red liquid. You smell the liquid; it appears to be a mixture of fruit juice and what smells like brandy. You take the cup and give it to the evidence technician to process for prints and to analyze the liquid. You notice that the hand towels in the bathrooms are similar to the one found at the murder scene. Mrs. Townsend verifies that a hand towel is missing from room 322.

Registration Cards

At the same hotel, you and your partner look at the two registration cards and notice that they were filled out by two people. Each is signed Cheryl Claymore, but the signatures are clearly different. No address or car information is filled in. In addition, a Visa credit card receipt for $68.00 is attached to the cards.

Names _____   Date ____/____/____

_____

QUESTIONS - CHAPTER 2 CONTINUED

6. What important information did you receive from the cleaning lady?

7. What potential evidence did you collect from Ms. Townsend?

8. Explain the link between the hotel and the murder scene?

9. Why do you think the suspect(s) took a hand towel from room 322?

Names _____   Date _____/_____/_____

_____

QUESTIONS - CHAPTER 2 CONTINUED

10. Why were the registration cards filled out by two people? Who filled them out?

11. What do you do next?

   A. Go home since you have worked your eight hours?

   B. Continue calling people listed in Cheryl's address book to obtain background information on Cheryl? Explain.

   C. Drive to Suei Lee's house and interview her? Explain.

Telephone Calls

You and your partner knock on the doors of the hotel in hope of finding a witness. No one saw Cheryl Claymore or anyone who may have been with her or anyone acting suspiciously. You get a list of the hotel guests who had checked out prior to your arrival.

You get Ms. Lee's telephone number and call her. The person who answers the telephone says Lee is away but should return about 3:00 p.m.

You and your partner return to the police station and start looking through Ms. Claymore's address book. You call the first number you see. It belongs to A.J. Automotive; you speak with Mr. Oha, an employee. He tells you that Cheryl Claymore is married to A.J. Claymore and gives you A.J.'s telephone number. In addition, Mr. Oha says that Cheryl drives a newer black Mercedes Benz. You call A.J. and tell him you need to speak with him in person. He says he will be home all night.

Interview With Suei Lee

At 3:20 p.m. you and your partner arrive at Ms. Lee's home. She tells you she remembers that Cheryl Claymore and three males registered at the hotel about 3:00 a.m. Ms. Lee says that Claymore walked to the office window with a man in his mid-20's, 5'9", medium build, short black hair, clean shaven and friendly; he was wearing a white t-shirt. Cheryl was wearing a blue dress. The other males also wore white t-shirts. Ms. Lee further says she gave Claymore the key to room 322 after Cheryl filled out the registration card and provided her with a credit card. When Cheryl took the key, Ms. Lee explains, the man said, "We need another room for my nephews." Cheryl agreed. Lee tells you she then gave Cheryl the key to room 106, and that *she* filled out the second registration card for the lady.

In addition, Ms. Lee tells you she saw Ms. Claymore and the man walk toward the stairs that lead to the upper floors and saw the two nephews go into room 106. She describes the nephews as 15 to 16-year-olds, both about 5'8" tall (she has trouble judging height); one had a thin face and, possibly, silver in his teeth.

Ms. Lee adds that during the next hour, she saw the males run back and forth from room 106 to (she supposed) the upstairs room. An hour later (4:00 a.m.), Ms. Lee says, Cheryl, visibly upset, returned to the office window to check out. Ms. Lee tells you she asked Ms. Claymore if she was alright. Cheryl replied, "I'm in a hurry, I had an emergency phone call." Ms. Lee processed the payment and watched Cheryl drive away west on Colorado Boulevard in a small black Mercedes Benz.

After questioning Ms. Lee, you and your partner establish that Lee never switched on the telephones to either room. In addition, you discover that she ran into the nephew with the discolored tooth in front of the candy machine located by the doors leading to the stairway. This area is well lit.

Names _____   Date _____/_____/_____

_____

QUESTIONS - CHAPTER 2 CONTINUED

12. How has Ms. Lee helped you with the time sequence?

13. Do you have any suspects? Explain.

14. What questions did Ms. Lee answer concerning the registration cards?

15. What important information did Ms. Lee relate to you concerning the relationship of the suspects?

Names _____   Date _____/_____/_____

            _____

QUESTIONS - CHAPTER 2 CONTINUED

16. Will Ms. Lee be a good identification witness? Explain.

17. What part of Ms. Lee's statement verified a witness statement from the murder scene?

18. What unique physical feature, according to Ms. Lee, did one of the males have?

19. What do you do next?

    A. Notify A.J. Claymore of his wife's murder and interview him? Explain.

    B. Put off the notification and concentrate on identifying the suspects? Explain.

    C. Ask for background checks on all witnesses?

Interview With A.J. Claymore

N.C.I.C.: The National Crime Information Center (N.C.I.C.) is a national computer data base located in Washington D.C. and operated by the FBI. This system is used by law enforcement agencies; it contains investigative information such as stolen guns, stolen property, wanted persons and stolen vehicles.

At 5:05 p.m. you and your partner drive to Hawthorne to meet A.J. Claymore. There, you also meet Cheryl's sister, Wanda Claymore. Interestingly, Cheryl's maiden name is the same as her married name. You tell them about the murder.

A.J., who, is 64-years-old, reacts emotionally; he tells you that he and Cheryl were recently separated but had been married for four years. He says the last time he saw Cheryl was two days ago. He confirms that she drove a 190E black Mercedes Benz bearing a California plate that reads "A.J.s." He adds that she had an L.A. Cellular telephone in her car.

A.J. can't recall anyone in the city of Pasadena who knew Cheryl; however, he thinks it ironic that she and Mandi visited Pasadena last week to watch a cheerleading contest.

"Who is Mandi?" You ask.

"She's Cheryl's nine-year-old daughter by a previous marriage. He also tells you Mandi's last name is Parker and that the father lives somewhere in Los Angeles.

A.J. points to a child playing with toys and says, "This is Cheryl's and my three-year-old son, Landon." You smile and say hi to Landon and then ask about Mandi's whereabouts. "My God, I forgot about Mandi! I don't know where she is," A.J. tells you.

Names _____   Date ____/____/____

_____

QUESTIONS - CHAPTER 2 CONTINUED

20. What have you learned about Cheryl and A.J.?

21. A.J. confirmed that Cheryl drove a black 190E Mercedes Benz. Whose statements did he verify?

22. What important information did A.J. relate concerning the car?   Why?

23. What other information do you need from A.J.?

   A. Information about his business? Explain.

   B. Information regarding any life insurance policies, sons from a first marriage who may fit the suspects descriptions, small caliber guns that he may own? Explain.

   C. Information about his relationship with Cheryl's family? Explain.

24. At this point, what is your main concern? Explain.

A.J. Claymore—Further Information

A.J. tells you Cheryl works at Jefferson Mortuary in Los Angeles. He also tells you that it has been a long time since he and Cheryl have fought physically or even argued. In addition, he tells you the reason they separated was that Cheryl wanted to socialize and he didn't.

A.J. also says that he and Cheryl bought separate life insurance policies two years ago; each named the other as primary beneficiary. Each policy is worth $150,000.

Lastly, you determine that A.J. owns a .32 caliber Smith and Wesson revolver and a shotgun. He shows you the shotgun. The handgun, he says, is at his brother's house.

Before you leave, you ask A.J. if he has any grown sons from previous marriages.

"I've got five sons: Landon, three-years-old, A.J. Jr., 32-years-old, Keith, 30-years-old, Raymond, 29-years-old and Daniel, 28-years-old." He adds that Junior lives in Washington, Keith and Raymond live in San Bernardino and Daniel lives in San Francisco. In addition, A.J. tells you that none of his sons, or their families, have visited within the past six months.

Interview With Wanda Claymore

A.J. is out of the room when you interview Cheryl's sister. Wanda confirms his statements. She tells you that she has not spoken with Cheryl for a few days. It occurs to her that she doesn't know any of Cheryl's friends and so, unfortunately, she doesn't know where Mandi could be. She recalls, however, that Cheryl was to meet some friend Friday evening. You gather from the conversation that she and Cheryl were always on good terms but were not necessarily close.

Wanda calls her mother to see if, perhaps, Mandi is staying with her. She is not. The elder Mrs. Claymore says she doesn't know where Mandi or Cheryl might be. Wanda, who appears to have taken the news well, tells her mother about Cheryl's murder. Mrs. Claymore can easily be heard through the telephone line. Understandably, she is upset. Wanda tells her to "stay put," she'll be there soon after the detectives leave. The mother, however, insists on speaking to a detective. You take the phone.

Mrs. Claymore gets directly to point. She tells you that A.J. did it. "He killed my Cheryl for the insurance money." She adds that, "he chased my daughter around for weeks until she finally signed the papers—the same way he did to get her to marry him." She says more. You listen. When she is through you thank her for this information then hand the telephone back to Wanda. You look at your partner and sigh; he acknowledges that he got the gist of the conversation and he rolls his eyes. You both know, instinctively, that this is one mother-in-law who will have plenty more to say.

You ask Wanda to call you if she hears anything relating to the whereabouts of Mandi, or her sister's murder.

Names _____   Date _____/_____/_____

_____

QUESTIONS - CHAPTER 2 CONTINUED

25. What have you now learned about Cheryl's and A.J.'s disposition?

26. Why did you ask A.J. about guns?

27. Why did you ask A.J. about his sons from a previous marriage?

28. Was Wanda's statement useful? Explain.

Names _____   Date ____/____/____

_____

QUESTIONS - CHAPTER 2 CONTINUED

29. Does A.J. have a motive to kill Cheryl? Explain.

30. What do you do at this point?

    A. Immediately place Cheryl's car in N.C.I.C. as having been stolen and used in a homicide. Also, place Mandi's name in N.C.I.C. as missing and, possibly, as having been kidnapped? Explain.

    B. Ignore that Mandi is missing since that is for the juvenile section of the police department to handle? Explain.

    C. Talk to the life insurance company and the witnesses and tell them the status of your investigation.

N.C.I.C.

Before leaving A.J.'s apartment, you telephone the records section of the police department and speak to a cadet. You ask him to place Cheryl's car information in N.C.I.C. as having been stolen and used in a homicide. In addition, you have him place Mandi's name in N.C.I.C. as missing and a possible kidnapping victim.

Chapter 3

Finding Cheryl's Car

April 28 (Saturday) *continued*

Telephone Interview With Nina Brice

At 7:30 p.m. at the police station, you attempt to locate Mandi. She is your priority. In Cheryl's address book you come across the name, Nina Brice. You call her hoping she might be a possible link to Mandi.

Nina tells you that she and Cheryl are close friends as well as business partners. She explains that they operate a lingerie modeling forum and sell lingerie.

Nina says she saw Cheryl three nights ago when she, Cheryl and Mandi met for dinner. She tells you that during dinner Cheryl burst into tears and complained that A.J. had been ignoring Mandi and when he did acknowledge her, he did not treat her well. Nina says that Cheryl decided—that night—to file for divorce.

Nina adds that Cheryl recently met a man at her work and was supposed to go out with him last night. In addition, you discover that Cheryl kept in touch with Mandi's grandmother but not with Mandi's biological father. She had not seen him in years. You and your partner continue calling numbers in the address book to locate Mandi, but no one has seen her.

Name(s) _____   Date _____ / _____ / _____

_____

QUESTIONS - CHAPTER 3

1. What line of business was Cheryl in?

2. What pieces of evidence, found at the hotel, make sense to you now?

3. Did Nina shed light as to why A.J. would want to murder Cheryl?

4. What information did you learn about Mandi's father? Why could this be significant?

5. Based on the investigation so far, what do you think happened?

Finding Cheryl's Car

Blood Spatter: When blood is forced out of the body it leaves a pattern on whatever it touches. Experts analyze and interpret these patterns and give opinions as to the position of the body when the wound was inflicted, what order the wounds were sustained and how much force created the wound.

At 10:30 p.m. you get a call from the Inglewood Police Department; they recovered Cheryl's car in front of 8907 South 3rd Street. The car is now at Brian's Tow. You and your partner drive to the towing agency and inspect the car.

The interior is full of scattered papers. The rear passenger seat, behind the driver, is soaked with blood. You find a .25 caliber bullet casing by the rear window; it is similar to the ones found at the crime scene. You find a clump of bloody hair between the rear seat and the back passenger door on the driver's side.

The keys are in the ignition so you turn the radio on and listen to the hard rock music playing. Your most important discovery is that the cellular telephone is missing. You arrange for the car to be towed to the Pasadena Police Department.

Name(s) _____   Date ____/____/____

_____

QUESTIONS - CHAPTER 3 CONTINUED

6. Is it significant that you found Cheryl's car in Inglewood?

7. The radio was tuned to a hard rock station. Is this significant?

8. What piece of evidence found in the car has a link to the murder scene?

9. What can you deduce from your inspection of the car? Explain.

10. What do you do after inspecting the car?

   A. Call it a night and go home? Explain.

   B. Go to where the car was found and interview the residents in the neighbor-hood? Explain.

   C. Inspect the car a second time just to be thorough? Explain.

April 29 (Sunday)

Cheryl's Car Continued

Around midnight you and your partner drive to 8907 South 3rd Street where the car was found. You wake several residents and talk with them about the car.

Interview With Carolyn Paxon

Mrs. Paxon tells you she saw the Mercedes Benz parked in front of her house between 10:30 a.m. and 11:00 a.m. yesterday (April 28). She adds that neither she nor her family heard or saw anyone who could be associated with the car. In addition, she tells you that no one touched the car. The other family members confirm this.

Interview With Tom Paine

Mr. Paine, who lives south of the Paxon's, tells you he noticed the car at 5:30 a.m. when he left for work. He says the car was not running but the front lights were on and no one was around. He, too, says he didn't touch the car.

Interview With the Gambles

At 1:00 a.m. your partner contacts the Gambles, an elderly couple in their 80's, who live across the street from Mr. Paine and the Paxons. Mr. Gamble tells your partner that he and his wife were awakened at approximately 2:00 a.m. (April 28) by a car horn. He adds that they both looked out their bedroom window and saw three males get out of the black Mercedes Benz and walk down the street to an El Camino. They got into "this second car," he describes as "lighter than black" and drove southbound on 3rd Street.

Call From Wanda Claymore

At 3:30 a.m. Wanda Claymore pages you. You call her. She says Mandi has been found. Apparently, Mandi was at Rochelle Moren's house, a friend of Cheryl's. Wanda adds that Rochelle called her this morning to tell her that Mandi was sick. She says that Rochelle told her that she and Cheryl were suppose to go out Friday evening, but Cheryl dropped off Mandi at her house, then went to the store and never returned. Rochelle told Wanda that she did not call her sooner because she thought Cheryl would return and, besides, Mandi and her daughter, Megan, were enjoying each other's company. When Mandi took ill with a bad stomach ache, Rochelle felt she should contact a family member. Unfortunately, Wanda did not get Rochelle's telephone number. You request that she get Rochelle's phone number and address when Rochelle drops off Mandi later in the day. You also instruct Wanda to ask Rochelle to page you.

Investigation Continues

At about 4:15 a.m. you and your partner return to the station. The two of you have been working almost 24 hours without sleep. Again, you go through Cheryl's address book and the name "Lawrence" catches your eye. There is a telephone number written next to the name and a notation, "South Pasadena." You look up the number in a criss-cross directory and find that Lawrence's last name is Wills. He lives in South Pasadena, a small city to the south of Pasadena, in an apartment complex less then a quarter mile from the place Cheryl's body was found. You and your partner discuss this coincidence.

Mountain Avenue and Page Place are somewhat remote and chances are good that residents are mainly responsible for drive-through traffic. This creates an interest in Lawrence. You and your partner are extremely tired and need to rest. You agree to get a few hours sleep and regroup at 9:00 a.m.

At 9:00 a.m. you and your partner meet at the station and begin supervising the evidence technicians who are processing the car. You make sure they photograph all sides of the car, internal and external. You also want pictures of the tire marks and the blood spatter.

The technicians collect the loose papers for fingerprinting. They fingerprint the entire exterior and those parts of the interior conducive to printing. You look into the trunk and glove compartment in hope of finding evidence that will help solve this case. You do this without a search warrant or consent from A.J. Claymore.

Chambers v. Maroney (1970) 399 U.S. 42

The United States Supreme Court ruled that a law enforcement official may search a vehicle without a warrant if there is probable cause to believe that it contains evidence of a crime.

Name(s) _____   Date ____/____/____

_____

QUESTIONS - CHAPTER 3 CONTINUED

11. What time sequence have you determined from the Inglewood residents witnesses' statements who live on 3rd Street?

12. Who are the most important witnesses you found on 3rd Street? Why? What makes them credible?

13. Whom do you need to contact immediately?

    A. Rochelle Moren? Explain.

    B. A.J. Claymore? Explain.

    C. Sergeant Sandoval? Explain.

14. Why is Lawrence Wills important?

Evidence Found in the Mercedes Benz

The evidence technicians find the following items:

1. Miscellaneous photographs of Cheryl, A.J. and Mandi - interior
2. Several loose papers with writing - interior
3. Many pieces of lingerie - trunk
4. Four sets of key rings with keys attached - glove compartment
5. Single key with a plastic tag - possibly a motel key (not from the Mercury Motel) - interior
6. Plastic baggie with a small amount of marijuana - interior
7. Envelope containing $250.00 - trunk
8. Envelope containing $500.00 - trunk
9. Envelope containing several checks issued to Jefferson Cemetery - trunk
10. Life insurance policy - trunk
11. Blood scrapings - interior (rear passenger seat area)
12. Hair - interior (rear passenger seat area)

The interior and exterior portions of the car are fingerprinted; one palm and two partial fingerprints are found. The quality of the prints is not good enough to identify the person(s) through a computer search. According to your department's fingerprint expert, they can only be matched if the person(s) is identified and prints are submitted for comparison.

While reviewing the life insurance policy, you notice that the policy limit is $250,000—double indemnity. A.J. Claymore is the beneficiary. He will inherit $500,000 from Cheryl's murder.

Interview With Mrs. Noud

At 12:00 p.m. you and your partner drive to 1744 City Street, the apartment complex where Lawrence lives. His name is not on the mailboxes so you stop at the manager's apartment. Mrs. Noud, the manager, tells you Lawrence's apartment number is 201 but says he has already left for the day. Lawrence, she says, is in his early 30's, a muscular man. She adds that he has been in trouble. She recalls that he recently lost his temper over the use of the pool—he yelled and was out of control (almost broke down her door when she refused to address her complaints).

Mrs. Noud also tells you that she noticed Lawrence has been driving his father's grey El Camino. She also noticed his nephew, a tall (about 6'2"), thin 15-year-old is visiting, and that he has been hanging around with Lawrence for the past week.

You and your partner knock on Lawrence's door to verify her statements. No one answers. You check his designated parking space in the complex's garage. It's empty.

Call to A.J. Claymore

You and your partner return to the police station. You call A.J. and speak to him about the $250,000 insurance policy found in Cheryl's car. He apologizes for his failure to mention that they raised their policy limits from $150,000 to $250,000 two months ago. Upon hearing the news of Cheryl's murder, he says, he forgot.

Telephone Message - Rochelle Moren

At 2:00 p.m. Rochelle Moren calls you. She has just spoken with Wanda. She whispers and sounds scared. She tells you that she wants to meet but not at her home. You arrange to meet her tomorrow at 2:00 p.m. outside her office. Moren verifies that she and Cheryl were going to go out Friday evening but that Cheryl left to go to a store and never returned. You try to get more information by telephone but she insists you meet tomorrow instead.

"Why?" you ask.

"I may know who killed her."

Name(s) _____   Date ____/____/____

_____

QUESTIONS - CHAPTER 3 CONTINUED

15. What would you consider to be the most important pieces of evidence found in the Mercedes Benz? Explain.

16. What is your feeling about the discrepancy regarding the life insurance policy?

17. Are you satisfied with A.J.'s response regarding the above policy?

18. Is Lawrence Wills a suspect? If so, what is his motive?

Name(s) _____   Date ____/____/____

_____

QUESTIONS - CHAPTER 3 CONTINUED

19. What link is there between Lawrence Wills and the murder suspects?

20. What was Rochelle Moren's most important statement to you?

21. Should you wait or should you go to Rochelle Moren's house now? Explain.

Jefferson Cemetery

At 3:00 p.m. you and your partner drive to Jefferson Cemetery, where the victim worked, and meet Michael Mantel, a co-worker. He is a tall man in his forties, well over 6 feet tall. He tells you that he last spoke with Cheryl the morning of April 27 about depositing company cash and checks into the bank. He assures you that he did not set up a date with Cheryl for the evening of April 27 or 28. He also assures you that he was not having a relationship with her. Michael tells you he is the only male working at the cemetery.

Michael asks you about the checks and cash that Cheryl was supposed to deposit. You tell him that you found both and, in a few days, after you inspect the currency more closely you will turn everything over to Jefferson Cemetery.

At the cemetery, you get paged and call the number. It's Deadra Brown, a friend of Cheryl. She tells you she may have information about Cheryl's death. You make an appointment to meet her later that afternoon at her apartment.

Nina Brice called you earlier to say she has some information about Lawrence. You and your partner drive to Nina's work for the interview.

Nina Brice ~ 2nd Interview

At 3:00 p.m. you and your partner meet Nina at a hair salon. She tells you Lawrence once lived in Pasadena and that he owes Cheryl $6,000. Nina says he was Cheryl's lover and that Cheryl lent him money to help him with his acting career. She further tells you that Cheryl was waiting for Lawrence to get a job so he could pay her back; however, Lawrence kept putting her off. Cheryl, she said, threatened to sue Lawrence a week ago.

"Why didn't you tell us this before?"

"I was scared."

You also learn from Nina that even though Cheryl's children were the most important part of her life, Cheryl liked to socialize at nightclubs. She stated adamantly that Cheryl never used drugs.

Interview With Deadra Brown

At 4:30 p.m. you and your partner meet Ms. Brown at her apartment in Hawthorne. She tells you that on April 28, at about 5:45 p.m., she and a friend were leaving the parking lot at their school when they were almost hit by a man driving a black Porsche. She says he stopped, apologized and introduced himself as "Vaughn." Deadra adds that they talked and, since he seemed nice, she gave him her telephone number.

Earlier today, Vaughn called and asked if she wanted to go to lunch; she accepted. He got "take-out" and brought it to her apartment. She noticed that while they ate, Vaughn kept staring at the picture of Cheryl that she keeps on the mantle. She explains that Vaughn said, "You know, a funny thing happened to me. I met a girl on Friday (April 27) and she got killed that same day. The girl dropped her daughter off at a babysitter and left to get some candy, but never returned. Her body was found in Pasadena and her car was found in Inglewood."

Deadra also tells you that, soon after, Vaughn used her telephone and called a friend. She overheard him say, "If that was you, why did you get into something you couldn't handle?" Ms. Brown tells you she did not think much about Vaughn's comments because she had not heard of Cheryl's death; however, the connection clicked in her head when Nina told her about Cheryl's death.

You learn that Vaughn is about 21-years-old, 5'11", thin and wears prescription glasses. When he met Deadra for lunch he wore a white t-shirt and green pants. You ask Deadra to call you if Vaughn contacts her.

"Try to find out his last name and where he lives," you say.

"I'll try."

When you and your partner return to the station, a message is given to you; it states that Cheryl's autopsy will take place tomorrow at 10:00 a.m.

Name(s) _____   Date _____ / _____ / _____

_____

QUESTIONS - CHAPTER 3 CONTINUED

22. Would you consider Michael Mantel a suspect? Explain.

23. How did Mantel help answer questions concerning some evidence found in the car?

24. What new information from Nina Brice peaked your interest?

25. Are you satisfied that Cheryl was not a drug user? Why? Why not?

26. What is your feeling about Vaughn? Explain.

27. Based on your investigation so far, who would you consider as possible suspects? What are their motives? Explain.

Chapter 4

The Autopsy

April 30 (Monday)

Telephone Interview With L.A. Cellular Company

Search Warrant: An order by a judge commanding a law enforcement official to search a person or property for specified item(s) which tends to establish that a crime was committed and identifies who committed the crime. In order for a judge to sign the warrant, the law enforcement official, the affiant, must show probable cause through an affidavit that establishes grounds for the issuance.

Probable Cause: Probable cause is an accumulation of articulated facts that would lead a reasonable person to believe that a crime has been committed.

Before leaving to the coroner's office, you telephone L.A. Cellular and speak with Patti Zucker. She tells you she needs a search warrant in order to turn over any information regarding Cheryl's car telephone records. You expect this and ask how long it will take for them to give you the phone records after they receive the warrant. She answers, "10 days."

Subsequently, Ms. Zucker looks at the cellular records and says that she could, with the permission of Mr. Claymore, reconstruct the billing cycle and get the information within seven days. Ms. Zucker adds that since Mr. Claymore is named in the contract with L.A. Cellular, they could provide him with the information.

You get A.J. on the phone; he agrees to give Ms. Zucker permission. Zucker contacts you and says that she'll call you as soon as the records are available. You thank her and decide to pass on a search warrant.

Autopsy of Cheryl Claymore

Autopsy: The Coroners Office has jurisdiction over bodies whose death results from a violent or suspicious manner. An autopsy, an internal and external examination of a body conducted by a deputy medical examiner, is conducted to determine the cause and approximate time of death. Based on the examination, the medical examiner determines whether death was "at the hands of another," suicide, accidental or of natural causes.

At 10:00 a.m. you and your partner drive to the coroner's building in Los Angeles. Inside the clothing room, you gown-up in paper clothing that covers your clothing, hair, mouth and shoes. In the autopsy room, six autopsies are under way.

Cheryl's body is at the end of the room. Dr. Lisseana is attending to it. He tells you that Cheryl was shot *five* times in the head and shows you X-rays. Four bullets were recovered. During the examination you see the holes in Cheryl's skull.

Description of Gunshot Wounds

Tattooing: When a gun is fired, gunpowder is emitted from the weapon. If someone is shot at close range (within 12 inches) gunpowder will burn and implant into the skin of the victim around the entry wound. This effect is known as tattooing.

Gunshot Wound #1

This entry wound is located at the top of the head. The bullet's path is slightly left to right and downward. The projectile—a small caliber, copper jacketed, lead bullet—is recovered just inside the skull; it never penetrated the brain. Tattooing is present which indicates that the gun was either touching the skin or extremely close to the skin when it was fired.

Gunshot Wound #2

This entry wound is located at the top of the head about a half-inch from wound #1. The bullet's path was slightly left to right and downward. The projectile—two fragments of a small caliber, copper jacketed, lead bullet—is recovered just inside the skull; it never penetrated the brain. Tattooing was present.

Gunshot Wound #3

This entry wound is located near the right temple. The bullet's path was slightly back to front, right to left, and very slightly downward. The bullet exited near the left cheek. The bullet fractured several bones and punctured the pituitary gland. Tattooing was present at the entry wound. This was the fatal wound, however, death was not instant.

You ask the doctor to better detail the path of the bullet. He takes a long thin metal rod and inserts it in through the entrance wound, through the skull, and out the exit wound. He leaves the rod in place, so you can follow the path of the bullet when it entered the skull. Thus, with this information, you know where the gun was positioned.

Gunshot Wound #4

This entry wound is located at the left cheek near the exit wound of gunshot wound #3. The bullet's path was left to right and downward. The projectile—a small caliber, copper jacketed, lead bullet—is recovered from the left side of the lower jaw. Tattooing was not present.

Gunshot Wound #5

This entry wound is located behind the left ear. The bullet's path is back to front, left to right, and sharply downward. The projectile—a small caliber, copper jacketed, lead bullet—is recovered in the right side of the chin. The bullet traveled through the muscle and tongue; it fractured the jaw.

The doctor tells you it appears Cheryl was a very healthy woman. He makes an incision to the left forearm of Cheryl and inspects the wound. There is no sign of drug use as you earlier suspected. Rather, it is his opinion that the paramedics attempted an I.V. (Later, you confirm this with the paramedics.)

You and your partner are also told Cheryl was wearing a menstrual pad. Doctor Lisseana advises that the toxicology tests and his report will be completed in a few weeks.

You collect the bullets, Cheryl's clothing, the menstrual pad, a sample of her blood, the trace evidence from the sexual assault examination (seminal stains) and take them to the Los Angeles County Sheriff Department's Crime Lab for serology and firearms testing. This chain of custody is usually handled by the coroner's employees, but you and your partner opted to do it because you want to speak with the experts about the case.

20 F

Multiple Gunshot wounds to head.
No tattoos are noted.

CLAYMORE CHERYL.

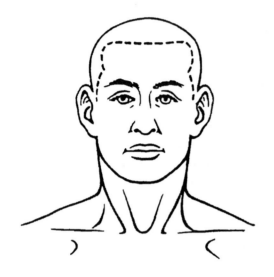
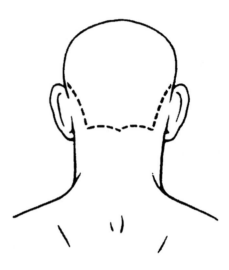

Gunshot wounds #1 and #2
Entry wounds.
Soot is present.
No stippling.
No Exit.

Gunshot wound
#3 Entry wound.
No stippling
Soot is present
on the dura mater of
the right temple.

Gunshot wound
#3 Exit.

Gunshot wound
4 Entry wound.
Neither Soot nor Stippling is present.
No Exit.

Gunshot wound
#5 Entry wound.
No Exit
Neither Soot nor Stippling
is present

_____ M.D.
Deputy Medical Examiner.

768372C

20

Multiple Gunshot wounds to body. (Head).
See Form 20F.

Claymore. CHERYL
DOD 4-28-XX   69
HOMI
PASADENA P.D.

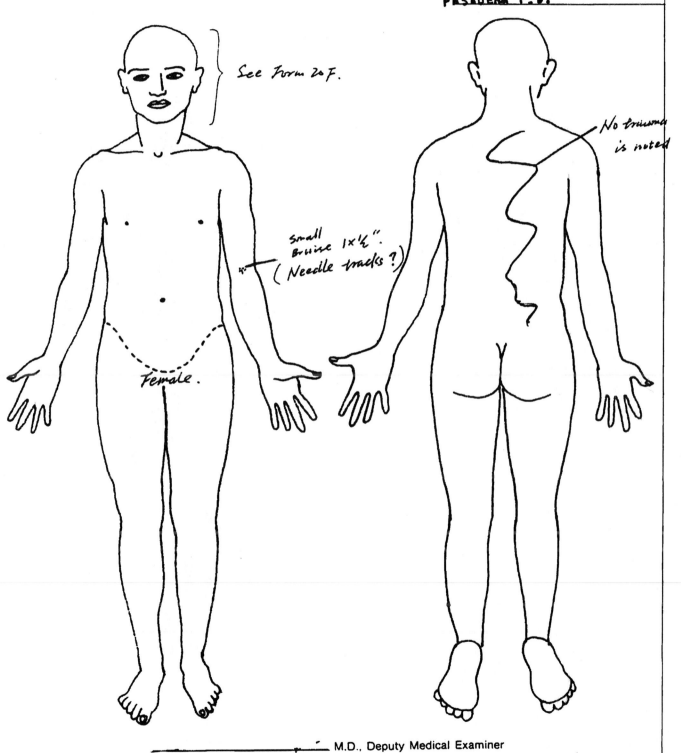

See Form 20F.

No trauma is noted

Small Bruise 1×½".
(Needle tracks?)

Female.

_____ M.D., Deputy Medical Examiner

(5) Multiple Gunshot wounds to head.

CLAYMORE, CHERYL

fractures of the left Maxilla of
The track of GSW #4.

Fractures of
the right inner
mandible of the
GSW #5.

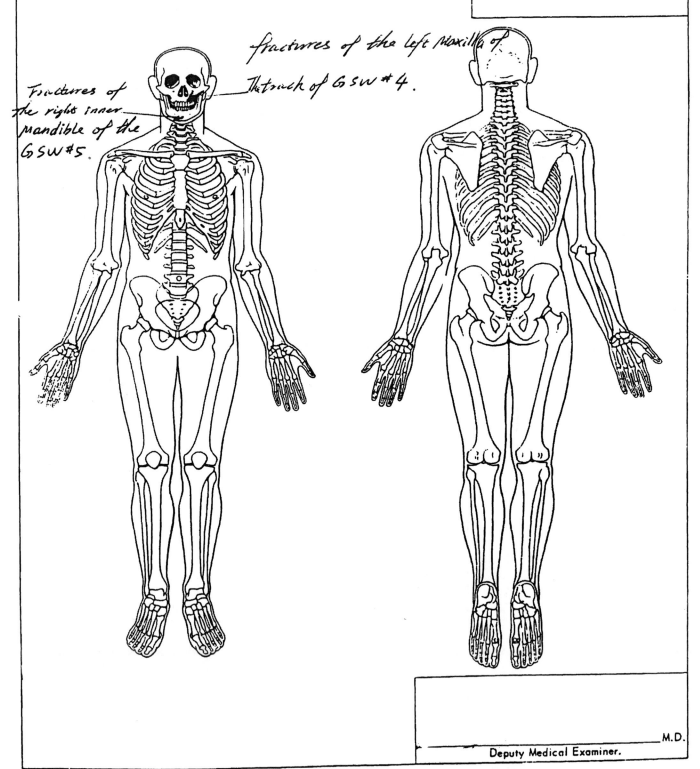

_____ M.D.

Deputy Medical Examiner.

76B372B

20G

Multiple Gunshot wounds to Head.
(5).

CLAYMORE, CHERYL

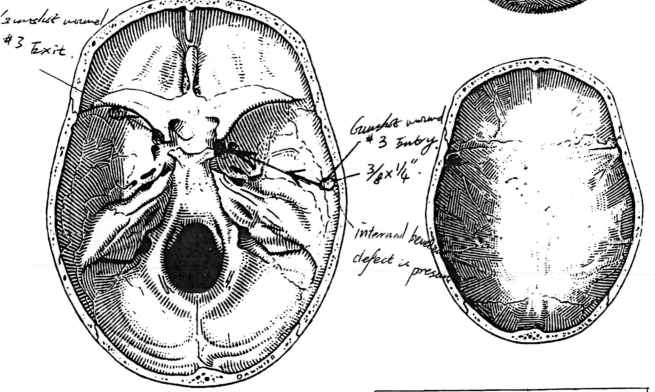

Gunshot wound
#1 entry wound.
1/2 x 3/8 "

Gunshot wound
#2 Entry.
3/8 x 1/4 "

Internal
bevelled
defect
is seen

Gunshot wound
#3 Exit.

Gunshot wound
#3 Entry.
3/8 x 1/4 ".

internal bevel
defect is present

_____ M.D.

Deputy Medical Examiner.

20 D

(5) Multiple Gunshot wounds to Head.

CLAYMORE, CHERYL

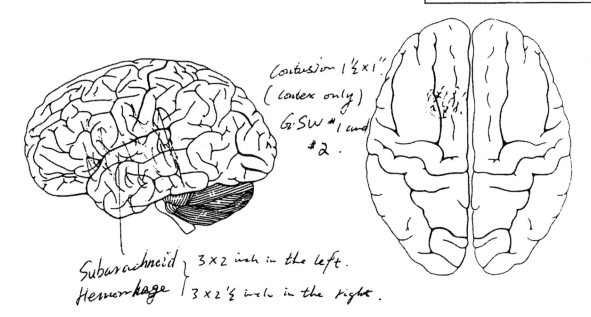

Contusion 1½ x 1"
(cortex only)
G.S.W #1 and
#2.

Subarachnoid } 3 x 2 inch in the left.
Hemorrhage } 3 x 2½ inch in the right.

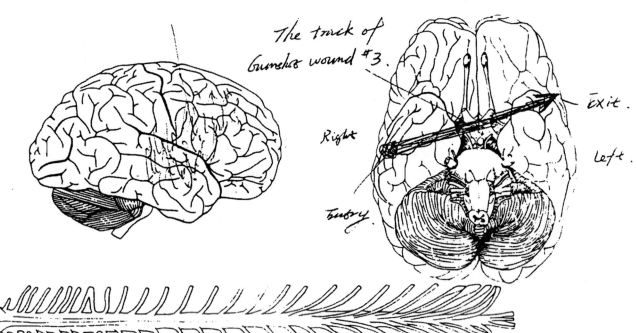

The track of
Gunshot wound #3.

Right

Exit.

Left.

_____ M.D.
Deputy Medical Examiner.

81

☒ Complete Procedure — Kit # __10 6 6__

☐ Modified Procedure

Initiated as a Special Processing Case by:.

Coroner's Investigator _____

Date: __4/28/XX__   Time: __0830__

Location: ☐ FSC   ☒ At Scene ☐ Other

CC# _____

Decedent's Name __Claymore Cheryl__

☐ Male   ☒ Female

EVIDENCE COLLECTION STARTED: Date: __4/28/__ Time: __1842__

		AT SCENE	AT FSC	COLLECTED BY	NOT COLLECTED	NONE SEEN
1.	PHYSICAL EVIDENCE collected from body surfaces _____ *	☐	☐	DA	☐	☒
2.	EXTERNAL STAINS collected _____	☐	☐	DA	☐	☒
3.	BITE MARK(S) processed _____ *	☐	☐	DA	☐	☒
4.	TOOLMARK(S) processed _____ *	☐	☐	DA	☐	☒
5.	NIPPLES swabbed _____	☐	☒	DA	☐	
6.	PUBIC HAIR combed _____	☐	☒	DA	☐	
7.	EXTERNAL GENITAL area swabbed/two smears made _____	☐	☒	DA	☐	
8.	ORAL CAVITY swabbed/two smears made _____	☐	☒	DA	☐	
9.	RECTUM swabbed/two smears made _____	☐	☒	DA	☐	
).	VAGINA swabbed/two smears made __2 Sets of Swabs__	☐	☒	DA	☐	
11.	VAGINAL LAVAGE collected _____	☐	☒	DA	☐	
12.	PENILE SHAFT swabbed/two smears made __NA__	☐	☐		☐	
13.	BODY SURFACE CONTROL collected (Location __Left Ankle__)	☐	☒	DA	☐	
14.	HAIR STANDARDS collected _____ *	☐	☒	DA	☐	

☐ Head   ☐ Facial   ☐ Chest   ☐ Arm   ☒ Pubic

| 15. | NAIL SAMPLES collected _____ * | ☐ | ☒ | DA | ☐ | |

☒ Clippings   ☐ Scrapings   ☐ Damaged nail(s)

EVIDENCE COLLECTION COMPLETED: Date: __4/28/XX__   Time: __1915__

OBSERVATIONS AND COMMENTS: * not enclosed in kit

Panty Hose & Panties were intact: Menstrual pad found inside
    of panties

Reviewed by DME prior to autopsy:.

Deputy Medical Examiner _____ M.D.   Date: _____ Time: __1/r__

WHITE: TO BE PLACED WITH MEDICAL PAPERS PRIOR TO AUTOPSY.

CANARY: TO ACCOMPANY KIT TO EVIDENCE ROOM.

PINK: TO BE ENCLOSED IN KIT.

82

- ☐ Probable Accident
- ☐ Probable Suicide
- ☐ Questionable Suicide/Possible Homicide
- ☑ Probable Homicide
- ☐ Homicide Investigator Requests Rush

Kit # 15073

Claymore, Cheryl
DOD 4-28-
HOMICIDE 69
Pasadera P.D

- ☐ Male   ☑ Female

INFORMATION ABOUT DECEDENT/SHOOTING

- ☐ Right Handed   ☐ Left Handed   ☑ Unknown

Occupation ___UNK___

Activity Prior to Shooting ___UNK___

Have the decedent's hands been touched by anyone prior to taking the GSR sample? ☑ Yes ☐ No
If yes, by whom? ☑ Paramedics ☐ Family ☐ Police ☐ Hospital Personnel
☐ Other ___

Was the weapon found in the decedent's hand? ☐ Yes ☑ No
If yes, which one? ☐ Right ☐ Left
If no, describe weapon's location in relationship to decedent's hands ___

Shooting Occurred: ☐ Indoors ☑ Outdoors ☐ Unknown

Location of Body: ☐ Indoors ☑ Outdoors ☐ Automobile ☐ Hospital
Other ___

Number of Shots Fired: ___3___

Date ___4-28-___ and Time ___0300___ of Shooting

Date ___4-28-___ and Time ___0845___ GSR samples were taken.

GSR evidence collected ☑ At Scene ☐ At FSC ☐ At Hospital
☐ Other ___ By: ___

Body transported to FSC via ☑ Coroner's vehicle ☐ MTS

FIREARM

- ☐ Revolver   ☑ Semi-automatic/automatic   ☐ Rifle   ☐ Shotgun

Other (e.g., Derringer, Single shot pistol, etc.) ___

Made/Model ___UNK___ Caliber ___UNK___

AMMUNITION

Brand of Ammunition ___ Type of Ammunition ___

Bullet Configuration: ☐ Round Nose ☐ Hollow Point ☐ Wad Cutter ☐ Pointed

Other ___

Bullet Surface: ☑ Jacketed ☐ Semi-jacketed ☐ Bare Lead ☐ Plated

Comments: ___

___ ___Investigator___ ___4-28-XX___ Date

— Do not write below this line —

RESULTS:

Bullet wt: ___

Barrel Length ___

Name(s) _____   Date ____/____/____

_____

QUESTIONS - CHAPTER 4

1. Why did you opt to have Mr. Claymore request the telephone records from L.A. Cellular rather than getting a search warrant?

2. What new finding was revealed at the autopsy?

3. Which shot that Cheryl sustained was the fatal wound? Explain.

4. What have you learned from the autopsy?

Name(s) _____   Date _____/____/_____

_____

QUESTIONS - CHAPTER 4 CONTINUED

5. What do you think was the sequence of the shots?

6. Why did you have the doctor use the metal rod to probe the head?

7. What did you learn about the alleged drug use?

Chapter 5

Rochelle Moren

Interview With Rochelle Moren

At 2:30 p.m. you and your partner meet Rochelle Moren at her work. The three of you drive to a McDonald's Restaurant get drinks and talk about the case.

Ms. Moren tells you she became friends with Cheryl Claymore several months ago; they met at Jefferson Cemetery. (A relative died.) Coincidentally, both had young daughters and they also became friends.

Rochelle says that on April 27, at about 8:00 p.m., Cheryl and Mandi arrived at her home on 3rd Street in Inglewood. Rochelle and Cheryl were going to a nightclub. Their daughters were to spend the night with Rochelle's father.

Rochelle adds that she and Cheryl talked and played with the girls until she went to her room to dress. At about 10:00 p.m. Cheryl told her that she was going to the liquor store to get snacks for the girls. She left in the Mercedes Benz and never returned.

Rochelle admits that she was angry with Cheryl when she did not return because she felt Cheryl had "stood her up"— Cheryl had done this before. Rochelle explains that at other times when they made plans, Cheryl sometimes failed to show. But she was never a "no show" when Mandi was involved. When Cheryl did not call or return by Sunday morning, and when Mandi got sick, she became concerned and called Wanda. That is when she learned of Cheryl's death.

Ms. Moren says she believes that a neighbor, a 20-year-old gang member named Cecil McKnight, might be responsible. She tells you that Cecil met Cheryl Friday evening (April 27) when she arrived with Mandi. Rochelle describes Cecil as a "womanizer" and says he commented to Cheryl something like, "I'd love to have you." Ms. Moren tells you that Cheryl got a little angry and told Cecil to "grow up." Ms. Moren adds that Cecil stared angrily at Cheryl as she walked away.

You discover that Cecil is about 5'10", thin and sometimes wears glasses. In addition, she tells you that a younger gang member hangs out with Cecil to prove his gang worthiness. She only knows the kid as "Romeo" and describes him as 14 to 16 years of age, about 5'8" and thin.

You question her further and learn that Cecil's favorite drink is a mixture of fruit punch and brandy. Rochelle fixes this when he visits. She also tells you that Cecil likes marijuana.

You and your partner drive to Wood's Liquor—it is three blocks away from Ms. Moren's house. The employee tells you that Mr. Chang, the owner, was working late on Friday (April 27). He is currently out of town and will be back tomorrow. You drive to a second liquor store, nearby, and show the employee, who was working Friday evening, a picture of Cheryl, but he does not remember her.

Name(s) _____   Date _____/_____/_____

_____

QUESTIONS - CHAPTER 5

1. What information did Ms. Moren give you regarding time sequence?

2. Was Rochelle's explanation about delaying her call to Wanda reasonable?

3. Is Cecil McKnight a suspect? Explain.

Name(s) _____   Date _____/_____/_____

_____

QUESTIONS - CHAPTER 5 CONTINUED

4. What other information did Ms. Moren provide which interested you?

5.   What do you do next?

   A. Interview Cecil McKnight? Explain.

   B. Contact Ms. Moren's neighbors and try to find out Romeo's true name? Explain.

   C. Contact Inglewood Police detectives and see if they have information on McKnight and Romeo, as well as photographs? Explain.

Tuesday (May 1)

Meeting With Inglewood Police

At 10:00 a.m. you meet with homicide detectives and gang officers of the Inglewood Police Department. You learn Cecil McKnight also goes by the name Vaughn McNeil. You confirm that he lives across the street from Rochelle Moren. You also confirm he is a "leader" in a well established gang in Inglewood. No information can be found regarding Romeo, but you get a photograph of McKnight. In addition, the gang officer tells you that Cecil has a brother, Kevin McKnight, a 13-year-old about 5'7", thin with very short hair, but no photograph is available. He is also part of the gang. You ask if they have fingerprint cards on Cecil or Kevin; none can be found. You also establish that McKnight lives in the Morning High School District.

Name(s) _____   Date ____/____/____

_____

QUESTIONS - CHAPTER 5 CONTINUED

6. What is your feeling about Cecil McKnight having an aka Vaughn McNeil? Is he the same person Deadra Brown met?

7. Why do you have an interest in Romeo and Cecil McKnight's brother, Kevin?

8. Why did you get a photograph of McKnight?

9. Why did you inquire about the school district?

2nd Meeting With Deadra Brown

With Cecil McKnight's photograph in hand, you and your partner drive to Deadra Brown's apartment. You show her the picture. She identifies McKnight as the person she met, who is also known as Vaughn.

Interview With Mr. Franks

At 1:00 p.m. you speak with Mr. Franks, Dean of Discipline at Morning High School. Franks escorts you and your partner to his office. Inside, hanging on a wall, are two life size posters of professional basketball players, Byron Scott and Elden Campbell. You point them out. He tells you they attended Morning High before joining the Los Angeles Lakers. Franks is a nice man and, for a while, you find the trivia interesting, but you need *current* information and put him back on track. You ask him about Romeo. He knows Romeo, he says, then changes the subject. He expounds on his success coaching basketball players and takes credit for their professional accomplishments. Eventually, Mr. Franks says that Romeo's true name is Joe Mitchum. He is 15 years old, 5'8", thin, clean shaven and possibly has a gold or silver front tooth, maybe braces. He adds that Mitchum was expelled from Morning High because of discipline problems that stemmed from gang relations. "He fought a lot during the infrequent times he attended school." Mr. Franks tells you Mitchum is now enrolled in Morning Alternative School in Inglewood. You and your partner have enjoyed Mr. Franks' company. You thank him and excuse yourselves—quickly. You rush to Morning Alternative but are told that Mitchum has been suspended for two weeks, and, they say, they cannot release Mitchum's home address without a warrant.

Recontact With Inglewood Police

Booking Photograph: After a person is arrested and before the suspect is processed into jail, a booking photograph of the suspect's head and chest is taken for identification purposes. The suspect's name, the date and the assigned prisoner number is affixed to a plate that is placed in front of the suspect's chest prior to the booking photograph.

You and your partner return to the Inglewood Police Department to see if they have any information regarding Joe Mitchum. They give you a recent booking photograph. Mitchum was arrested a month ago for possession of marijuana.

Later, when you return to your police station, you discover that Joe Mitchum used to live in Pasadena. He was arrested there two years ago for carrying a firearm at a school. As it turned out, however, the firearm was merely a starter's pistol, similar to those used in track meets.

Interview With Mr. Chang

At 6:00 p.m. you and your partner drive to Wood's Liquor and meet Mr. Chang. You show him a photograph of Cheryl; he remembers her. He tells you Cheryl came into the store at about 10:00 p.m. and purchased a pint of Hennessy Brandy, two pastries, possibly another item, but he could not remember. He adds that she was alone. He also noticed that she drove up in a black Mercedes Benz.

Mr. Chang tells you that he did not see anyone in the parking lot, either before or while Cheryl was in the store. He looks at Cecil's and Joe's photographs. Cecil McKnight, he says, comes into the store often. He does not remember seeing Joe Mitchum.

Recontact With Suei Lee

Photo lineup: A photo lineup is used to identify a possible suspect. It is shown to an eye witness who may identify a suspect involved in the crime. Also known as a "six-pack," a photo lineup usually consists of six booking photographs of individuals with similar features.

Photo lineup admonition: Before an officer shows a witness a photo line-up, the officer admonishes the witness. This admonition advises the witness that, "You are under no obligation to identify anyone. We want the guilty person identified but we also want innocent persons cleared of any suspicion. Just because we are showing you photographs does not mean that the guilty party is among those individuals shown." The witness must acknowledge his/her understanding of the admonition, and if a positive identification is made, the witness must sign and date the back of the photograph of the person identified.

You and your partner return to the police station and put together two photo lineups—one with Joe Mitchum's picture, the other with Cecil McKnight's picture. At 9:30 p.m. you contact Ms. Lee and show her the lineups after admonishing her regarding lineups.

Ms. Lee immediately points to Joe Mitchum's picture and says he was one of the nephews. She is positive of her identification because she saw him under the lights by the candy machine. She adds that he is the one with the silver tooth. This confirms your information. Ms. Lee looks at the photo lineup with Cecil McKnight's picture. She cannot identify him.

Name(s) _____   Date ____/____/____

_____

QUESTIONS - CHAPTER 5 CONTINUED

10. What information did Mr. Franks provide which is consistent with Ms. Lee's statement?

11. What information did you receive from the Inglewood officer about Joe Mitchum that peaked your interest?

Name(s) _____   Date _____/_____/_____

_____

QUESTIONS - CHAPTER 5 CONTINUED

12. What information did you discover about Joe Mitchum that is important?

13. Did Mr. Chang help you with the time sequence? Explain.

14. Is the information regarding what Cheryl purchased at the store important?

15. Ms. Lee said that Joe Mitchum was one of the three males with Cheryl Claymore. Is this credible?

Name(s) _____   Date _____/____/____

_____

QUESTIONS - CHAPTER 5 CONTINUED

16. Based on what you know so far, answer the following questions:

Who are your suspects?

What happened regarding this crime?

When did these crimes occur? (time sequence)

Where did the events happen?

Why was Cheryl murdered? (motive)

How was Cheryl allegedly abducted, raped, and robbed and how was she killed?

Name(s) _____   Date ____ / ___ / ____

_____

QUESTIONS - CHAPTER 5 CONTINUED

17.   What do you do next?

A. Arrest Cecil McKnight for Cheryl's murder? Explain.

B. Obtain a search warrant, search Mitchum's residence and arrest him for
    Cheryl's murder? Explain.

C. Arrest the entire Inglewood gang for Cheryl's murder and search the city of
    Inglewood for evidence?

May 2 (Wednesday)

At 8:30 a.m. you begin preparing a search warrant for Joe Mitchum's residence. Your partner has gone to Inglewood to *confirm Mitchum's current address. You finish the search warrant and wait for your partner to return.

* Before serving a warrant you must confirm the person's address so that you don't go barging into the wrong person's house and scare the heck out of them.

May 3 (Thursday)

Nighttime Endorsement: A search warrant, signed by a judge, must be served within 10 days between the hours of 7:00 a.m. and 10:00 p.m. A nighttime endorsement allows law enforcement officers to serve search warrants between 10:00 p.m. and 7:00 a.m. The affiant—the officer who writes the affidavit of the search warrant—must convince the judge that service, between 10:00 p.m. and 7:00 a.m., is justified. Nighttime endorsements are most prevalent in narcotic search warrants.

Your partner confirms Joe Mitchum's residence. In fact, your partner discovers that Joe paid the rent to the landlord yesterday. You walk to the courthouse and meet Municipal Court Judge Michaels. The Judge reads your warrant, signs it and commands you to search Mitchum's residence for the following items:

1. A .25 caliber semi-automatic pistol

2. A portable cellular telephone

3. Any clothing belonging to Joe Mitchum that may establish evidence of the crime

4. Any vehicle that may be in possession of Joe Mitchum

Judge Michaels also commands you to search the person of Joe Mitchum. In addition, your request for nighttime service is approved. (See Search Warrant.)

Note: During your investigation, you have kept in contact with Cheryl's mother and sister. You have spoken to them by telephone, in person, and you have provided them general updates regarding the investigation.

Chapter 6

Interrogation and Interview

May 4 (Friday)

Joe Mitchum's Interrogation

Knock and Notice: Penal codes state that when police or officials serve warrants, they must knock and give notice to the residents of the property to be searched. The "door man," the officer assigned to give the knock and notice, will go to the door, knock and listen. If someone answers, the officer will identify himself/herself and will enter with other officers. If no one answers, the officer will give notice, "Police department, open up we have a warrant." After waiting, usually a minute or so, and after continuing to give knock and notice, and if no one answers, officers will force their way into the property. However, when officers knock, give notice and hear running they will force entry in order to stop the suspect(s) from fleeing or destroying evidence.

Interrogation: Formal questioning of a suspect that is designed to obtain incriminating statements regarding his/her connection with the crime being investigated.

***Miranda* Rights:** These are rights of persons in *custody*. They involve the Fifth and Sixth Amendment rights against self-incrimination and right to counsel. *Miranda* includes the following rights:

1. Right to remain silent
2. Anything you say can and will be used against you in a court of law
3. You have the right to an attorney and to have the attorney present during questioning
4. If you can not afford an attorney, one will be provided to you at no cost

   If suspects understand their rights and wish to talk with an officer, then their statements are valid evidence and can be used in court.

With the assistance of the Inglewood Police officers, who surveil Joe's apartment and confirm he is there at 2:00 p.m., you, your partner and other detectives from the Pasadena Police position yourselves by the door. You knock. Mitchum answers. Your team enters. Mitchum is handcuffed. He is the only person present.

You give him a copy of the search warrant (not the affidavit) to review, pursuant to the law (see following search warrant and affadavit).

Mitchum blurts out, "That f_ _ king Sly!"

You and the detectives search the apartment; you take an address book, a pair of gloves with red stains and a white t-shirt. None of the items listed on the search warrant are found.

You arrest Joe Mitchum for murder and transport him to Pasadena's Jail. The only discrepancy you find is that Mitchum does not have a silver tooth; however, he tells you that "Sly" does. Mitchum, however, has a front tooth that protrudes and is discolored.

You and your partner escort Mitchum to an interview room; the conversation is recorded. You read him his *Miranda* Rights; he tells you he understands and is willing to waive them. Mitchum is shown a picture of Cheryl Claymore. He denies knowing her or ever meeting her, adds that he has not been in Pasadena in over eight years and that he has never been to a hotel. He is adamant that he did not shoot Cheryl and wants to know what girl identified him. You ask him how he knows the eyewitness is a female. He does not respond.

Mitchum tells you that at 8:00 p.m. on Friday, April 27, he was with a friend named Damon. At 10:00 p.m., he says, Damon dropped him off at home and he was there the rest of the night. Mitchum tells you that from 10:00 p.m. to 2:00 a.m. he was on the telephone speaking to girls he knew; however, he cannot remember exactly which girls he spoke to.

You and your partner remind Mitchum that two years ago he took a weapon to a school campus and was arrested by the Pasadena Police. Mitchum argues that it was four years ago—not two.

Eventually, Mitchum tells you he was on 3rd Street, in Inglewood, the evening of the 27th visiting Cecil McKnight but cannot remember the exact time. In addition, when you ask about his uncle, "Sly," he tells you Sly's been in trouble a lot for drugs and just got out of prison. Mitchum says Sly is 22 years old, 5'10" and thin, and his real name is Brian, but he cannot remember his exact last name. When you press him about his uncle's last name, he decides he doesn't want to speak to you anymore.

With help from gang officers at Inglewood Police station, you determine that Sly's first name is Quintin, not Brian as Mitchum said, and that his last name is Slide. Mitchum, however, calls his uncle, Sly. In addition, Sly has a silver front tooth. They have, however, no booking photograph.

Later, you contact Mitchum's guardian to tell her about the search and arrest. The concerned grandmother verifies Mitchum's statement. Mitchum *was* home by 10:00 p.m. on April 27. You and your partner transport him to Juvenile Hall, in Los Angeles; he will stay there pending a criminal filing by the district attorney's office and a court trial.

You submit Mitchum's fingerprints to the fingerprint expert for comparison to prints found on Cheryl's car. No match is found. This means that Ms. Lee's identification will be extremely important unless other evidence surfaces.

STATE OF CALIFORNIA - COUNTY OF LOS ANGELES

(DUPLICATE/ORIGINAL) SEARCH WARRANT

THE PEOPLE OF THE STATE OF CALIFORNIA TO ANY SHERIFF, POLICEMAN OR PEACE OFFICER IN THE COUNTY OF LOS ANGELES: proof by affidavit having been made before me by

___Detective XXXXXXXXXX___ that there is probable cause to believe that the property described herein
(Name of Affiant)

may be found at the locations set forth herein and that it is lawfully seizable pursuant to Penal Code Section 1524 as indicated below by "x" (s) in that it:

___X___ was stolen or embezzled

___X___ was used as the means of committing a felony

_____ is possessed by a person with the intent to use it as a means of committing a public offense or is possessed by another to whom he or she may have delivered it for the purpose of concealing it or preventing its discovery.

___X___ tends to show that a felony has been committed or that a particular person has committed a felony,

_____ tends to show that sexual exploitation of a child, in violation of P.C. Section 311.3, has occurred or is occurring;

YOU ARE THEREFORE COMMANDED TO SEARCH:

XXXXXX XXXXXXXXX, apt #16: This location is a multi-story apartment building on the south side of XXXXXXXX Street between Crenshaw Avenue and Parkway Vista in Inglewood. The apartment building is light brown with dark brown trim. The numbers XXXXX are clearly displayed on the front of the building. Apartment #16 is situated on the second level at the southwest section of the building. The number 16 is clearly marked on the apartment door.

The person of Joe Mitchum, a male, with the birthdate of xx/xx/xx. Joe Mitchum stands 5'9" tall, 130 lbs and possibly has a silver or gold tooth or braces. Joe Mitchum lives at the above address.

FOR THE FOLLOWING PROPERTY:

1. .25 caliber semi-automatic pistol, unknown make or model
2. Portable cellular telephone, unknown make or model
3. Clothing, including but not limited to, shoes, shirts, pants, jackets or any other article of personal effects belonging to Joe Mitchum which would establish, or tend to establish, evidence of the crimes addressed in the affidavit
4. Any vehicle in the possession or control of Joe Mitchum

AND TO SEIZE IT IF FOUND and bring it forthwith before me, or this court, at the courthouse of this court. The Affidavit in support of this Search Warrant is incorporated herein and was sworn to this _____ day of _____ , 19 ____ , at _____ A.M./P.M. Wherefore, I find probable cause for the issuance of this Search Warrant and do issue it.

_____ , NIGHT SEARCH APPROVED: YES [   ] NO [   ]
(Signature of Magistrate)

Judge of the Superior/Municipal Court, _____ Judicial District

DATE AND TIME OF SERVICE OF WARRANT: _____

DA-1514-A—76T294S—8-86

AFFIDAVIT

Your affiant has been a police officer for over nine years, during this time he has participated in the investigation of several violent crimes including murder. I have been assigned to the detective section, crimes against persons, of the Pasadena Police Department since February 19xx. I have investigated numerous violent crimes, including homicides, attempted homicides, assaults and robberies, and have formal training in these areas. Your affiant received formal training in homicide investigations through the Los Angeles County Sheriff's Academy and the District Attorney's Homicide Symposium.

On April 28, 19xx at approximately 6:00 a.m. your affiant was called to Mountain Avenue and Page Place, in the City of Pasadena, to investigate a murder. Upon my arrival, I observed the dead body of a female lying in the middle of the street. This girl had been shot several times in the head with small caliber bullets. Two .25 caliber shell casings were found near the body. The victim was identified as Cheryl Claymore who resided at 615 Star Avenue, apartment 41, Hawthorne.

Your affiant was directed to the Mercury Hotel in Pasadena regarding a purse found on the premises. The purse had identification belonging to Cheryl Claymore. It was determined that Ms. Claymore had rented two rooms at this hotel at 3:00 a.m. on April 28, 19xx. According to Suei Lee, a hotel employee, Ms. Claymore was accompanied by three males. Ms. Lee described one male as being in his 20's, a little shorter than Ms. Claymore who stands 5'10", thin, short black hair, clean shaven and friendly. She described another male as a 14 to 16-year-old, 5'8", thin and possibly had silver in the teeth. The third male was described only as a teen-ager.

2

Ms. Lee explained that Ms. Claymore and the first described male initially rented room #322. The male then requested a second room. He was assigned room #106. Ms. Lee said she watched the males run between rooms for the next hour. At 4:00 a.m., April 28th, Ms. Claymore returned to the front desk to check out. Ms. Lee felt something was wrong because Ms. Claymore appeared disheveled. Ms. Lee asked, "Are you alright?" Ms. Claymore answered, "Yes, I had an emergency call." Ms. Claymore entered a black Mercedes Benz with the males and drove west on Colorado Boulevard.

At 4:20 a.m., 20 minutes after the Cheryl and the males left the hotel, residents in the area of Mountain Avenue and Page Place heard gunshots. One person saw a black car speed away. A short time later, Ms. Claymore's body was discovered in the middle of Mountain Avenue.

Your affiant discovered a cup with reddish liquid, which appeared to be a mixture of fruit juice and brandy in room 322 of the Mercury Hotel. This became significant after interviewing Rochelle Moren.

Ms. Moren, a friend of the deceased and resident of Inglewood, California, told me that she and Ms. Claymore had planned to go out the evening of April 27th, however, at about 10:00 p.m., Cheryl went to buy snacks for the kids and never returned.

Ms. Moren explained that a neighbor, Cecil McKnight, met Cheryl the evening of April 27th and made the comment, "I'd like to have you." Ms. Claymore was angered and told Cecil to "grow-up." Ms. Moren added that Cecil is a gang member who enjoys a drink she fixes, a mixture of fruit juice and brandy. Ms. Moren also indicated that Cecil has a close friend, a young male named "Romeo" who is also a gang member. Your affiant spoke to

3

Mr. Franks, Dean of Discipline at Morning High School, who
identified "Romeo" as Joe Mitchum. He described Mitchum as a 15-
year-old, 5'8", thin with possibly a silver or gold tooth or
braces.

Your affiant obtained a prior booking photograph of Joe
Mitchum, from the Inglewood Police Department, and put together a
photo line-up with Mitchum's picture and five other photographs.
This line-up was shown to Ms. Lee. She positively identified Joe
Mitchum as one of the three males who checked into and left the
Mercury Hotel with Ms. Claymore.

We also spoke with Ms. Deadra Brown, a friend of Cheryl
Claymore's, who met a male the day after the murder who
identified himself as "Vaughn." Vaughn was later identified as
Cecil McKnight. He told Ms. Brown, who was unaware of Cheryl's
death at the time, that he met a girl the other night who drove
to a liquor store, was abducted and, later, shot in the head in
Pasadena. This information is significant because it had not been
released to the press. Ms. Brown described Vaughn as 21-years-
old, 5'11", thin, clean shaven with short hair. He also wore
prescription glasses.

With help from the Inglewood Police personnel, your affiant
has verified that Joe Mitchum currently lives with his
grandmother at the address indicated on the search warrant.

Based on the facts stated in this affidavit, your affiant
requests a search warrant be issued to search Joe Mitchum's
residence as well as his person. It is your affiant's opinion,
based on his experience and training, that items listed on page 1
of the warrant will be found at the residence of Joe Mitchum and
will be needed to establish the identities of the person(s)
responsible for murdering Cheryl Claymore.

4

In addition, your affiant requests a nighttime endorsement so he can continue the murder investigation without delay. The seriousness of this crime is such that the apprehension of the suspect is important to public safety.

Name(s) _____   Date ____ / ____ / ____

_____

QUESTIONS - CHAPTER 6

1. Why did you read Mitchum his Miranda Rights?

2. Which of Mitchum's statements peaks your interest?

3. You taped Joe Mitchum's interrogation. Why?

4. What physical discrepancy of Mitchum concerns you?

May 5 (Saturday)

Lawrence Wills' Interview

Interview: When officers speak to *witnesses* or *victims* about their knowledge of the crime.

At 7:00 a.m. you and your partner meet at the station to begin writing your investigative reports. You plan to submit them to the juvenile deputy district attorney on Monday.

At 7:30 a.m. you get a call from Lawrence Wills; he called you the night before so this is not an unexpected call. He says he wants to talk. He'll be there at 8:00 a.m. You look forward to talking with him. It's a beautiful spring day, you've had your coffee and donuts and are looking out of your second floor window when he drives up in a blue Chevrolet El Camino. Seeing this, you take the stairs two-at-a-time and greet him at the street curb, all the while looking past him—at his El Camino.

Inside, in an interview room that is wired for sound to tape your conversation, you thank him for voluntarily coming to the station to speak with you and your partner.

You tell Wills about the murder and, initially, he tells you that he doesn't know Cheryl Claymore. When you place a photograph of her on the table in front of him this *jars* his memory. He apologizes to you for lying. He's scared, he says. When he has calmed down, Lawrence says he has known Cheryl for a year but hasn't seen her in four months. He adds that the last time he spoke to Cheryl was three weeks ago when she called from her work. The call was purely social. Mr. Wills admits that, a while back, he borrowed $3,500 from Cheryl to further his acting career. He insists they never argued about the money he owed her because she wasn't in a hurry to get it back. He adds that he doesn't know anyone in the Inglewood area. He agrees to be fingerprinted (Wills' prints are later compared to the prints found on Cheryl's car but no match can be made.) He also lets you inspect his car. You look for traces of blood but find nothing. For the sake of thoroughness, however, you photograph his car. Before he leaves, he gives you his nephew's name, birthdate and where he lives.

Name(s) _____   Date _____/_____/_____

_____

QUESTIONS - CHAPTER 6 CONTINUED

5. Why are you curious about Lawrence Wills' car?

6. Why didn't you read Wills his *Miranda* Rights?

7. Why thank Wills for voluntarily coming to speak with you?

8. Is Wills a suspect in this case?

Name(s) _____   Date _____/_____/_____

_____

QUESTIONS - CHAPTER 6 CONTINUED

9. Do you believe Wills? Why? Why not?

10. What do you think about Wills' nephew?

11. Why request fingerprints from Wills?

12. Do you have cause to arrest Wills for murder?

May 7 (Monday)

Criminal Filing on Mitchum

Criminal Filings: At the completion of successful criminal investigations, investigators document their findings in report form and submit it to deputy district attorneys. The filing deputy reviews the report and makes one of three decisions:

1. Reject the case
2. Reject the case pending further investigation
3. File the case

Filing deputies reject the case when it is their opinion that the case does not meet the elements of the crime or they feel that the crime could not be proven to a jury. Sometimes filing deputies will reject the case but feel the case warrants a criminal filing if further specific investigative steps are accomplished. Filing deputies file cases if they feel that a deputy district attorney can prove the elements of the crime to a jury. The case alleging the crime(s),is written by the filing deputy and typed in specific form by his or her staff, and then taken to the clerk's office and officially filed.

At 9:00 a.m. you and your partner go to the juvenile district attorney's office with your written reports. They tell you they will review them today; however, based on your verbal report to them (on Friday, May 4), they are ready to file a murder charge against Joe Mitchum.

Name(s) _____   Date _____/_____/_____

_____

QUESTIONS - CHAPTER 6 CONTINUED

13. What factors did the district attorney's office most likely rely on to file criminal homicide charges against Mitchum?

14. Is A.J. Claymore still a suspect? Explain.

15. Is Lawrence Wills still a suspect? Explain.

16. Is Cecil McKnight still a suspect? Explain.

Chapter 7

The Cellular Trail

May 7 (Monday)

Call From Patti Zucker

Pretext: It is legal for a person, such as a law enforcement officer, to intentionally mislead someone to obtain certain information, however, over-use may be detrimental to an investigation.

At 10:00 a.m. Patti Zucker, from L.A. Cellular, calls. She has the list of telephone numbers called from the evening of April 27 to the morning of April 28 and asks if you are interested in driving across town to pick it up.

A half hour later you learn that 17 calls were made: three on April 27 and 14 on April 28.

All three calls made on April 27 were over a minute in length. (Calls showing a minute on the billing report indicate that either connections were made but the calls lasted less than a minute **or** calls were attempted but no connections were made.) One call, made at 10:49 p.m., was to a Los Angeles number for two minutes. A second call, made at 10:53 p.m., was to a Gardena number for seven minutes. A third call, at 11:03 p.m., was made to Texarcana, Texas and lasted five minutes. (All the calls were made after Cheryl's abduction.)

Your partner calls the California numbers under the pretext that he is a representative of the telephone company. The residents tell your partner their names, family members' names, ages and addresses.

A 15-year-old at the second residence, Lisa Reece, seems the likely recipient of the phone call. Your partner spoke to an adult who said she lives alone with her daughter and is in bed by 9:00 p.m.; however, her daughter gets calls at all hours. This makes her mad and she would prefer that boys call at a decent hour but understands that kids will be kids. Nice lady. Seems receptive. This is important because it is a seven minute call, and it may link you directly to the murder suspects.

Your partner contacts Mr. Jones at the first residence, the one where a call came in at 10:49 p.m. He has a daughter, Sheryl, the same age as the Reece girl.

Your partner is confident he can pull-off the same pretext on the residents in Texas; he makes several attempts, but no one seems to be home.

Name(s) _____   Date _____/_____/_____

_____

QUESTIONS - CHAPTER 7

1. Why did you use pretext to gather information?

2. Of the three calls, what call is potentially the most important and why?

3. What do you do now?

    A. Interview Lisa Reece and Sheryl Jones? Explain.

    B. Let L.A.P.D. detectives interview Reece and Jones because they live in Los Angeles? Explain.

    C. Tell Lisa Reece and Sheryl Jones about the murder and name them as possible accomplices.

May 7 (Monday)

Lisa Reece Interview

At 5:25 p.m. you and your partner meet Lisa Reece, the 15-year-old school girl who, according to records, was telephoned by someone using Cheryl's cellular phone. She tells you she can't remember specifically what telephone calls she received on the evening of April 27. You know immediately this could be a problem. She is a potential key witness. You have to peak her memory. First, you start with yesterday and talk about *all* the calls she received. It is evident that she is a popular 15-year-old; she received more calls in one night than you and your partner receive in a week. Nonetheless, you talk about the night before and the night before that. She remembers some conversations but continues to have memory lapses. All of the sudden she thinks out loud, "If I could only remember what I was wearing." You ask her what she means and she responds, "If I could remember what I wore when I was on the phone, then, I might remember the call."

Seconds later you're in her room. She opens her closet door. One by one you remove different clothes and show them to her. Exasperated, she whines, "no, no, no." You keep removing her clothing. She has a lot of clothing but, finally, (about 20 minutes later) on the floor, on top of a pile of other clothes, you find a pair of cutoff jeans. Lisa looks at the jeans. She smiles. "Keith Rattling called me that night. We go to the same school." Keith told her he was calling from a car phone. He and his "homeboys" were cruising around in a "Benz." Lisa adds that she heard a girl in the background tell someone to "shut up." She says that she asked Keith if the girl's parents minded her being out so late. He laughed, "We're taking her to a hotel." Right after that, Keith told Lisa he would call back the next day and hung-up.

Lisa tells you Keith is 17-years-old, pretty tall and big but not fat. She adds that he lives in Gardena and gives you his telephone number. She doesn't know Joe Mitchum AKA Romeo. You leave her house without telling her about the murder.

You and your partner head to the Jones' residence.

May 7 (Monday)

Sheryl Jones' Interview

At 8:00 p.m. you meet Sheryl Jones at her home. Sheryl, another 15-year-old school girl, tells you Keith Rattling called her home on April 27 and asked to speak to her cousin. She adds that Jamie wasn't home, so she talked with Keith for a few minutes—long enough to figure out, because of the unique background sound, that he was on a cellular phone. Sheryl, too, does not know Joe Mitchum alias Romeo. You leave Sheryl's house without telling her about the murder.

Name(s) _____   Date _____/____/____

_____

QUESTIONS - CHAPTER 7 CONTINUED

4. Why did you take so much time going through Lisa's closet?

5. Which of Lisa Reece's statements peaks your interest?

6. What effect did Sheryl Jones' statement have on your investigation?

7. What do you do now?

    A. Obtain a search warrant for Rattling's residence and arrest him for Cheryl's murder? Explain.

    B. Ignore Reece's and Jones' statements because you've already arrested Mitchum for the murder? Explain.

    C. Go to Juvenile Hall and release Mitchum from custody? Explain.

May 8 (Tuesday)

Search Warrant for Keith Rattling

At 7:00 a.m., at the police station, your partner prepares a search warrant for Keith Rattling's house and person. A detective from the Gardena Police Department calls and gives you Keith Rattling's current address.

Municipal Court Judge Argeens reviews your partner's search warrant (see following search warrant, affiant statement and exhibit). He signs it and commands your partner to search the residence and person of Keith Rattling.

May 8 (Tuesday)

Plan

You and your partner decide to serve the warrant the next day (May 9) at 7:00 a.m. You have a meeting with fellow detectives and formulate a plan on how to enter the house and, hopefully, find Keith Rattling.

Name(s) _____   Date ____/____/____

_____

QUESTIONS - CHAPTER 7 CONTINUED

8. What plan would you formulate for serving the search warrant?   Give specifics.

STATE OF CALIFORNIA - COUNTY OF LOS ANGELES

(DUPLICATE/ORIGINAL) SEARCH WARRANT

THE PEOPLE OF THE STATE OF CALIFORNIA TO ANY SHERIFF, POLICEMAN OR PEACE OFFICER IN THE COUNTY OF LOS ANGELES: proof by affidavit having been made before me by

<u>Detective XXXXXXXXX</u>   that there is probable cause to believe that the property described herein
(Name of Affiant)

may be found at the locations set forth herein and that it is lawfully seizable pursuant to Penal Code Section 1524 as indicated below by "x" (s) in that it:

___X___ was stolen or embezzled

___X___ was used as the means of committing a felony

___X___ is possessed by a person with the intent to use it as a means of committing a public offense or is possessed by another to whom he or she may have delivered it for the purpose of concealing it or preventing its discovery.

___X___ tends to show that a felony has been committed or that a particular person has committed a felony,

_____ tends to show that sexual exploitation of a child, in violation of P.C. Section 311.3, has occurred or is occurring;

YOU ARE THEREFORE COMMANDED TO SEARCH:

The residence at xxxxx xxxxxxxxx Street, City of Gardena, County of Los Angeles. The residence has a white stucco exterior with brown trim and a brick planter box next to the garage. The house is the third residence west of xxxxxxx Avenue on the north side of xxxxxxxxx Street. The numbers XXXX are clearly marked on the curb in front of the residence and also on the front porch post.

The person of Keith Rattling, a male with a DOB of xx/xx/xx. Keith Rattling is 5'10" tall and slim.

FOR THE FOLLOWING PROPERTY:

Firearms, ammunition, expended bullets and bullet fragments, expended shell casings, receipts for the purchase of arms and ammunition, bullet holes and blood stains (to be photographed, tested and excised if possible) and articles of identification tending to establish the identity of the person(s) in control of the described premises, such as rent receipts, utility receipts, addressed envelopes and keys, also, evidence needed in the normal course of a murder investigation, including but not limited to, photographs, letters, alcoholic beverage containers, food, ligatures, bite marks, or other biological material and an unknown brand cellular telephone.

AND TO SEIZE IT IF FOUND and bring it forthwith before me, or this court, at the courthouse of this court. The Affidavit in support of this Search Warrant is incorporated herein and was sworn to this _____ day of _____ , 19 ____ , at _____ A.M./P.M. Wherefore, I find probable cause for the issuance of this Search Warrant and do issue it.

_____ , **NIGHT SEARCH APPROVED: YES [**   **] NO [**   **]**
(Signature of Magistrate)

Judge of the Superior/Municipal Court, _____ Judicial District

DATE AND TIME OF SERVICE OF WARRANT: _____

DA-1514-A—76T2945—8/86

AFFIANT STATEMENT

Your affiant, a police detective, has been employed by the Pasadena Police Department for the last 10 years. During the past nine months, your affiant has been assigned to the Crimes Against Persons unit, during which time your affiant has investigated homicides, attempted murders, assaults, rapes and other crimes of violence. In addition to training at Rio Hondo Police Academy, your affiant has attended numerous post-graduate classes and seminars dealing specifically with the investigation of violent crimes. Your affiant is thoroughly familiar with the manner and means by which suspects commit violent crimes and their tendencies to retain the respective weapons used during the commission of the crime.

Your affiant is currently investigating a homicide involving the use of a firearm and the taking of a cellular telephone and has readily considered the attached police report bearing Pasadena case number xxxxxxxx, consisting of 2 pages, attached herein and referred to as Exhibit #1. Despite the lapse of time between the commission of the crime and the anticipated search, it is the opinion of your affiant, based on training and experience, that the weapon used in this homicide, described as a .25 caliber semi-automatic pistol, can still be located at xxxx xxxxxxxxxxx Street in the City of Gardena, County of Los Angeles. It is your affiant's further opinion, based on training and experience, that suspects frequently hide a firearm used in a crime inside their residence, in vehicles or on their person.

It is your affiant's opinion that finding the above described firearm and portable cellular phone, owned by the victim, is vital evidence in this case and will provide further proof to the identities of individuals responsible for this homicide.

It is your affiant's opinion, based upon the facts contained herein, that evidence pertaining to this case will be found at the above listed location.

Your affiant therefore prays that a search warrant will be issued.

EXHIBIT #1   page 1 of 2

VICTIM: SUSPECT:

Claymore, Cheryl   Rattling, Keith

Narrative:

On April 28, 19xx, Investigator xxxxxxxxxxx and I were detailed
to the scene of a homicide that occurred in the City of Pasadena.
The victim was a 26 year old female who was subsequently
identified as Cheryl Claymore. The victim was discovered on
Mountain Avenue, a small street at the south end of the city. The
victim was found clothed and had suffered numerous gunshot wounds
to the head. An intensive investigation was launched by these
investigators as to the identity of the suspects in this case.

As the investigation progressed, supported by statements from
Rochelle Moren, the victim's friend, it was determined that the
victim had been possibly abducted from a liquor store in the
Inglewood area of Los Angeles County by three males. The suspects
drove the victim to unknown locations and eventually arrived at a
hotel in Pasadena at approximately 3:00 a.m. on April 28th, 19xx.
Once at this hotel, the victim was forced to rent two rooms. An
hour later, the suspects and the victim left the hotel in the
victim's vehicle. The suspects then drove to the area of Mountain
Avenue and Page Place where the victim was shot five times in the
head.

During the course of this investigation it was learned from the
victim's husband that the victim had a cellular telephone
installed in her car. When the car was discovered abandoned in
Inglewood, the cellular telephone was missing. The victim's
husband, at the request of these investigators, immediately
requested the call logs for the cellular telephone through the
phone company. Our investigation determined that the victim was
abducted at approximately 2200 hours (10:00 p.m.) on April 27,
19XX, and upon receipt of the telephone logs, numerous calls were
recorded from 2207 hours (10:07 p.m.) until 2306 (11:06 p.m.) A
check of these telephone numbers revealed that most calls were
made to Los Angeles and Gardena. A check on several numbers
revealed the following information:

At approximately 2253 hours (10:53 p.m.), a call was made to
(xxx) xxx-xxxx. This number belonged to Lisa Reece who lives at
xxxx xxxxxxxx Street in Gardena. Miss Reece received a telephone
call from Keith Rattling. Miss Reece stated that he was talking
to her from a cellular telephone in a car. Reece added that
Rattling does not own a car, and she asked what he was doing.

EXHIBIT #1   page 2 of 2

Reece stated that Rattling told her he was with his "homeboys" and that they were taking a girl to a hotel. Reece said she heard a girl in the background tell someone to, "shut up." Reece estimated the female to be between 19 and 25 years of age from the sound of her voice. When Miss Reece questioned Rattling about the woman in the car, Rattling laughed and stated that he would call her back later.

In addition, Reece stated that Rattling called her back at about 0500 hours (5:00 a.m.) on April 28, 19xx, using the cellular telephone.

At approximately 1600 hours (4:00 p.m.) on June 6, 19xx, Investigator xxxxxxxxxxxxx and I contacted Sheryl Jones who lives at xxxx xxxxxxx in Los Angeles. Miss Jones had received a telephone call from Keith Rattling on April 27, 19xx at 2249 hours (10:49 p.m.) who was calling on a cellular telephone. Jones said that Rattling asked to speak to her cousin, Jamie. Jamie was not at home so Lisa spoke with Keith for a couple minutes. Miss Jones added that Rattling calls often but this was the first time he had called using a cellular telephone.

A check with the Gardena Police Department revealed that Keith Rattling lives at xxxxx xxxxxx Street in Gardena and his telephone number is (xxx) xxx-xxxx. Rattling was described as a male, 17 year-old, DOB of xx/xx/19xx.

The above facts, coupled with fact that the victim checked into a Pasadena hotel at 3:00 a.m. on April 28, 19xx, with three males (supported by hotel receipts) left an hour later then was shot to death 20 minutes after that, at 4:20 a.m., tend to show that Keith Rattling may be responsible, fully or in part, for the murder of victim Cheryl Claymore.

May 9 (Wednesday)

Search Warrant Served on Keith Rattling

You and your partner arrive at the station at 5:00 a.m. to review your plan and take care of last minute details. According to the plan, your partner will knock and give notice of the search warrant to whomever opens the door then let the other detectives, who have been briefed as to what to look for, take over the actual search. If Rattling is home, he will be taken into custody and be transported immediately to the police station.

At 7:00 a.m. you and the other detectives arrive at Keith's house and put the plan into action. Your partner goes to the front door and knocks. Keith Rattling's mother answers the door. Your partner identifies himself, gives notice and the officers enter and find Keith asleep in his bed. He is immediately handcuffed and walked to the police car.

Your partner explains the warrant in detail to Mrs. Rattling; she has no questions.

Meanwhile, in Keith's room, the focal point of the search, police find the following items:

1. Panasonic black cellular telephone - Cheryl Claymore's

    (Found under the bed)

2. Miscellaneous papers with gang graffiti and writing

    (Contained in a plastic box under the bed)

3. Miscellaneous gang photographs

    (Contained in a shoe box under the bed. The gang Rattling belongs to rivals Joe Mitchum's gang)

4. $115.00 in a black wallet along with two bindles of cocaine

    (Found under a dresser)

5. Pair of blue pants with red stains

    (Found in a closet)

6. Silver .25 caliber Raven semi-automatic handgun

    (Found under a dresser)

Name(s) _____   Date _____/____/____

_____

QUESTIONS - CHAPTER 7 CONTINUED

9. Why did you take Keith Rattling immediately to the police car?

10. What are the main items of evidence found in Rattling's house?

11. Why did you take the photo album?

12. What information since discovering gang photographs of Rattling concerns you regarding Joe Mitchum?

Chapter 8

Keith Rattling

May 9 (Wednesday)

Keith Rattling's Interrogation

Elements of a crime: According to the penal code, every crime has specific elements which must be proven beyond a reasonable doubt in order for a person to be found guilty of the alleged offense.

Murder (first degree)

1. Unlawful killing
2. Of a human being
3. With malice aforethought
4. Willful, deliberate or premeditated or
5. By poison, lying in wait, torture, in the commission of a burglary, arson, robbery, rape or mayhem

Kidnapping

1. Forcibly abducts a person and
2. Takes the person to another location

Rape

1. Act of sexual intercourse
2. Against the victim's will
3. Accomplished by force or fear with the capability of immediate unlawful bodily injury

Robbery

1. Taking of personal property
2. In possession of another
3. From the person or immediate presence
4. Against the person's will
5. By means of force or fear

On the way back to the station, you and your partner take Rattling to Mountain Avenue and Page Place. Neither of you say a word; you simply stop momentarily at the spot where the suspect(s) parked the Mercedes Benz the morning Cheryl Claymore was murdered, then continue on to the police station.

At 9:10 a.m. you walk Keith Rattling into the interview room; the tape has been set for the interrogation. You read Rattling his Miranda Rights. He says he understands his rights and wants to talk to you. You tell him you have a hell of a lot of evidence against him: the gun found under the dresser and the girl's cellular telephone. You put Cheryl's photograph in front of him. Beads of perspiration form on his forehead. His breathing becomes labored. He says nothing. You caution Keith that this will be the only time he will be able to talk to you about the case. You remind him about the gun and the telephone. He is a hard-core gang member at 17 years old, and seems to be "over his head." You wait.

He begins mumbling about the drive. You ask him to speak up. (You want his confession on tape *and* you want it audible.)

Keith says that on April 27 at about 9:00 p.m., he and Larounce Sands were driving in Larounce's gray El Camino in Inglewood when Larounce saw "the lady" walking into a liquor store. Larounce parked his car and said, "Watch this, I'm going to get this woman so we can do it to her." Larounce, AKA "Whack," took Keith's father's .25 caliber semi-automatic and walked to the girl's car. When the girl came out of the store, Larounce used the gun to force her into her black Mercedes Benz. Keith adds that Larounce drove the car with the lady in the front passenger seat to an unknown street in the area and that he followed. There, Keith says, they pulled to the curb and he got into the Mercedes, in the back passenger seat behind the girl. He adds Larounce said they were going to Pasadena.

Keith tells you they found a hotel and Larounce forced the girl to rent a room. When they were in the room, Larounce "did it to her." Keith says at some point they all left the hotel and drove back to Inglewood to check on Larounce's car. He explains that he and Larounce tried to drive back to the first hotel but couldn't find it. (Later he switched his story. He said he and Larounce, after leaving Inglewood, drove to Gardena and picked up their friend, "E-LOC," at Rowlins Park. Keith refuses to give you E-LOC's real name. You and your partner believe Keith is protecting a family member, possibly his older brother, but Keith adamantly denies this.)

Keith further tells you that on the drive back to Pasadena, he, Larounce, E-LOC and the girl tried to find the first hotel but couldn't remember its location. He says they decided to get two rooms at another hotel. One room was on the ground floor and the other on the third floor. He adds Larounce took her to the upstairs room first. He and E-LOC went up later and had sex with her. Keith also tells you that before leaving the hotel, he and Larounce went through the girl's purse in the parking lot and split thirty dollars.

Keith tells you he's feeling sick. You press on. He says when they left the second hotel that he drove the Benz, E-LOC was in the front passenger seat, Larounce was behind E-LOC, and the girl was behind the driver's seat. He adds Larounce told him to pull into an alley before getting onto the freeway to return to Inglewood. In the alley, Larounce said, "Tre-Nine"—a gang term for murder—then shot the girl in the head. He pulled her out of the car, then shot her some more. Keith closes by telling you they drove back to Inglewood, took the girl's cellular telephone and drove back home, to Gardena, in Larounce's El Camino.

Keith admits the cellular telephone found in his room was the girl's; he also admits the gun found is the one used to kill the girl. In addition, he tells you and your partner that E-LOC wiped down the hotel rooms and the car with a white wash rag from the hotel. He asks you if you know Detective Murphy from the Hawthorne Police. You answer that you don't know Murphy. You ask, "Do you want to speak with Murphy?" He nods.

Your partner calls Detective Murphy and briefs him about the murder and arrest. Murphy tells your partner that he knows Keith Rattling well and that Rattling and Larounce Sands are gang buddies and are generally together. Murphy agrees to speak with Keith, maybe get information about E-LOC.

Keith tells Detective Murphy that he is in deep trouble but that he didn't kill the girl; he blames the murder on Larounce. He tells Murphy he was truthful with the Pasadena detectives except for the part about the third guy—he didn't tell them E-LOC's real name. He admits to the detective that "Smoke" was the third guy. Since Murphy is not familiar with Smoke, Keith tells him that Smoke lives on Caster Street. Keith doesn't know the address, but the house is easy to spot because Smoke's red Cadillac is usually parked in the driveway. Detective Murphy asks if Smoke is Kevin Bryant. Rattling says he is, but he doesn't want to "rat," so he wants him to tell your partner Smoke's identity.

This is good information, but you wonder where Joe Mitchum fits in so you ask Rattling about Mitchum. He responds, "Never heard of him."

"What about A.J. Claymore or Lawrence Wills?"

"Don't know them either."

After you identify all parties you ask Rattling if he wants to ask any questions. He nods, "Can I go home now?"

You shake your head, "Not today."

You fingerprint your suspect and take him to Juvenile Hall in Los Angeles.

Name(s) _____   Date ____/____/____

_____

QUESTIONS - CHAPTER 8

1. Why did you and your partner drive Rattling by the murder scene?

2. Why did you put Cheryl Claymore's picture in front of Rattling during questioning?

3. What is of utmost importance when you read Rattling his *Miranda* Rights?

Name(s) _____   Date _____/_____/_____

_____

QUESTIONS - CHAPTER 8 CONTINUED

4. Why did you tape record Rattling's interrogation?

5. Did Rattling's statement seem credible? At what point did he seem to be protecting somebody? Explain.

6. What is "Tre-Nine" and why might this seem important?

7. What crimes did Rattling confess to? Explain.

Name(s) _____   Date _____/_____/_____

_____

QUESTIONS-CHAPTER 8 CONTINUED

8. What do you do now?

   A. Concentrate on finding more evidence against Rattling before focusing on Sands and Bryant? Explain.

   B. Focus on locating and arresting Larounce Sands and Kevin Bryant. In addition, contact the person in Texarcana and hope to identify Sands and Bryant from another source other than Rattling? Explain.

   C. Ignore Rattling's statement because you have Mitchum in custody? Explain.

Chapter 9

Texarcana Connection

May 9 (Wednesday)

Review of Telephone Records

Ms. Zucker of L.A. Cellular faxes you a complete copy of Cheryl's cellular telephone record—Cheryl's telephone was used 326 times from April 28 to May 7. You review these records and find that most are one minute contact time which typically indicates there was no answer. In addition, most calls are to the Gardena area.

From the information Rattling gave you about Sands, you discover that Larounce was arrested a week ago on a robbery warrant and is in custody at the Los Angeles County Jail. Bryant is not in custody and his whereabouts is unknown.

Late Wednesday evening, your partner again attempts to call the residents in Texarcana, Texas. (You record this conversation for him.) A young female answers and says she knows a lot of people in California because she used to live in Gardena. Your partner tells her that the telephone call in question was made about 11:00 p.m. on April 27 from a cellular telephone. She replies that she receives a lot of calls at night—too many to remember specifically.

Your partner suggests he give her a name or two. The girl says she knows Larounce Sands. She tells your partner that Larounce called and spoke to her and her cousin for about five minutes (this verifies the telephone record). She adds that the call came about 1:00 a.m., *Texas time*, on the 28th. (In California, this would be 11:00 p.m. on April 27.) Your partner asks for her name but, suddenly, the girl's mother grabs the telephone and wants to know why her teen-aged daughter is being questioned. Your partner continues with the pretext. The mother says, "We don't have a problem with our telephone charges," and hangs up. You call the Texarcana Police Department and request their assistance in identifying these occupants. Upon returning your call, they identify the occupants as the Andres family.

Name(s) _____   Date _____/_____/_____

_____

QUESTIONS - CHAPTER 9

1. Why did you tape record the conversation with the girl in Texas?

2. What information makes the girl's statement credible?

3. What is so important about this telephone call?

May 10 (Thursday)

Larounce Sands Interrogation

DNA: Deoxyribonucleic acid (DNA), like fingerprints, is a genetic pattern distinctive to individual human beings. With the exception of identical twins, each person's DNA is unique. Forensic scientists can determine a person's DNA pattern (genetic code) through blood, saliva and semen, and can match that code with a genetic code determined from evidence.

You and your partner drive to the jail and interrogate Sands.

Your partner hides a tape recorder in his jacket. The two of you go through the secured facility into the interview room. You decide on an enclosed room so you can have some privacy. After a while, Larounce Sands enters the room; he is 21-years-old, 5'8" and thin.

The recorder is turned on and you read Sands his *Miranda* Rights. He freely and voluntarily waives them and says he will talk to you without an attorney.

Surprisingly, Larounce says, "When I go on the witness stand do I gotta testify against the person that was with me?"

"Your lawyer will probably never put you on the witness stand unless you demand it," your partner responds.

You intervene. "We need to hear your side of the story. See, we have already spoken to your two friends and they're pointing the finger at you. We're not sure if you're the trigger man. We need to hear from you."

Larounce sits silently, stares at his hands resting on the desk, then at you. You paint a scenario that includes the liquor store and his grey El Camino.

"Maybe you're bullsh_ _ _ing me!"

You challenge his stare. "You called Texarcana, Texas."

"S_ _t, you really did your homework."

"So tell us what happened."

Larounce confesses that he and Keith Rattling were driving around in Inglewood, in his El Camino, when he saw a girl walk into a liquor store. He says he stopped, got out of his car and walked to the store's parking lot. When the girl came out and opened her car door, he walked up to her and said, "Get in." He denies using a gun.

You ask, "Why did she get into the car with you if you didn't use a gun?"

"I guess she was scared."

Larounce goes on to tell you that after the girl got into her car, he drove to "some" street and waited for Keith to park the El Camino. He says they were just driving around in the Benz when he decided to go to Pasadena.

"Why Pasadena?" You ask.

"I have nieces staying out there."

Larounce explains they drove to a hotel, but he forgot its name. You ask him to describe the hotel. He says he can't because he was pretty drunk. Larounce adds that he and the girl walked to the hotel desk. The girl paid for a room at the hotel and, both he and Keith entered the room with her.

"What was the number of the room?"

"I think it was 208."

Larounce tells you they just sat in the room; there was no sex. He explains he never had sex with the girl but maybe Keith did.

Your partner explains DNA to Larounce and tells him that they will be able to prove if he had sex with the girl.

Larounce thinks a bit, then tells you he had sex with her but not until later. He says Keith had the gun the entire night but the girl didn't know about the gun. Larounce adds they left the hotel and drove to Gardena to pick up Kevin Bryant at his home. He tells you Kevin got into the back seat with the girl and Keith rode in the front passenger's seat. Larounce says they tried to find the first hotel but couldn't, so they checked into another hotel and rented two rooms, one on the first floor and other on the third floor.

"Who checked into the hotel with the girl?" you ask.

"Kevin."

Larounce says Kevin went to the room on the third floor with the girl while he and Keith stayed downstairs. When Kevin was finished with the girl, Keith went to the room, then, after Keith was finished, he had the girl. He tells you she wanted to have sex with them.

"Don't you think she was scared to death and that's why she seemed willing to have sex?" You ask.

"Yeah I guess."

He tells you that just before they were ready to leave, Kevin told them that they had to kill the girl because she knew where he lived. Larounce tries to convince you that he was against that idea because he liked her.

He says, that before they left the hotel, he and Keith went through the girl's purse and took her money. He drove the car, Kevin was in the front passenger's seat, Keith was behind Kevin and the girl behind the driver's seat. He says that when he drove to an alley, Keith said, "Tre-Nine," and shot the girl in the head. ". . . he shot her in the head and I looked back and there was so much blood coming out of her. I said, 'ugh' and then he shot her two more times. She was lying in the back seat."

Larounce continues, "Keith and Kevin got out of the car, Keith opened the passenger door, and they threw the girl out. I heard two more shots after that."

Larounce adds they drove off, returned to Inglewood, dumped the Benz and got into his El Camino. Keith took the cellular telephone. He tells you they drove back to Inglewood the next day to burn the car so the police couldn't trace their prints, but the car was gone.

You ask him about Joe Mitchum, A.J. Claymore and Lawrence Wills. He doesn't know them.

Name(s) _____   Date _____/_____/_____

_____

QUESTIONS - CHAPTER 9 CONTINUED

4. How did the Texas call influence Larounce Sands' interrogation?

5. What are the similarities and differences in Rattling's and Sands' statements?

6. What do you do now?

   A. Get the criminal charges against Mitchum dropped and release him from custody? Explain.

   B. Locate and arrest Kevin Bryant for murder? Explain.

May 10 (Thursday)

Problem ~ Sands' Interrogation

Arraignment: A hearing in front of a judge after an arrest. At the arraignment the suspect, now referred to as the defendant, is told of the criminal charges and is appointed an attorney.

Impeachment: Impeachment is questioning the truthfulness of a witness' testimony in court because it appears contrary to that of a second witness. This second witness is often a police officer who testifies as to what was said to him/her which contradicts the first witness' testimony.

After Sand's interrogation you call the Gardena Police Department to get additional information on Sands. You speak with Detective Sean Conners. He tells you that he arrested Sands a week ago for robbery. In addition, Conners tells you he read Sands his *Miranda* Rights, but Sands refused to waive his rights and requested an attorney. You make another inquiry at the County Jail and discover that Sands is in jail for a weapons warrant and a robbery charge. You also discover that even though Sands was arrested a week ago, his arraignment for the robbery has been postponed and he hasn't been appointed an attorney.

McNeil v. Wisconsin (1991) 115 L Ed 2d 158

The United States Supreme Court ruled that if an officer takes a statement from a suspect in custody on an unrelated charge, the officer must inquire whether the suspect has waived his Miranda Rights on the unrelated charge; if he has, the officer must inquire whether the suspect specifically invoked his right to counsel. If the officer knows that the suspect has specifically expressed his desire not to speak without an attorney, the officer can still interrogate the suspect, however, only for purpose of impeaching his testimony at trial.

Name(s) _____   Date ____/____/____

_____

QUESTIONS - CHAPTER 9 CONTINUED

7. How does the *McNeil v. Wisconsin* ruling affect your case against Sands?

8. What have you learned from your mistake involving the Sands interrogation? Explain.

9. Can you eliminate A.J. as a suspect? Explain.

Name(s) _____   Date _____/_____/_____

_____

QUESTIONS - CHAPTER 9 CONTINUED

Can you eliminate Lawrence Wills as a suspect? Explain.

Can you eliminate Joe Mitchum as a suspect? Explain.

Can you eliminate Cecil McKnight as a suspect? Explain.

Name(s) _____   Date ____/____/____

_____

QUESTIONS - CHAPTER 9 CONTINUED

10. Based on what you know so far, answer the following questions:

   Who are your suspects?

   What happened regarding this crime?

   When did these crimes occur? (give the time sequence)

Name(s) _____   Date _____/_____/_____

_____

QUESTIONS - CHAPTER 9 CONTINUED

Where did the events happen?

Why was Cheryl murdered? (motive)

How was Cheryl abducted, raped, robbed and killed?

Loose Ends and Evidence

May 10 (Thursday)

Investigation - Post Sands' Interrogation

Ramey Warrant: A Ramey Warrant—an arrest warrant ordered by a judge based on probable cause—is not often used but is usually sought before the district attorney's office reviews the criminal investigation. The advantage of a Ramey Warrant is that the warrant can be put into N.C.I.C. for 30 days.

Sands' confession verified Rattling's confession with the exception of who shot the girl. It seems each knows the ramifications of being the "trigger man." You anticipate that learning the "truth" may be difficult or even impossible.

In their confessions, Sands and Rattling cleared Joe Mitchum, so you immediately contact the Juvenile District Attorney's office and request they drop the criminal charges filed against Mitchum. At Juvenile Hall, you request Mitchum's release. Later, you call Mitchum and apologize for the arrest. Mitchum seems unbothered and says, "That's okay." (You figure he was probably the topic of conversation among his friends and took credit for "beating" the case.) You also speak to his grandmother; she is not quite so obliging. "I want some answers, and they better be good," she says. You explain that Mitchum appeared connected to the crime by investigative leads, which you are not able to discuss, but that you and your partner believed he was involved when he was positively identified as one of the suspects. You have exonerated yourself and your partner to a point; the grandmother is satisfied—not elated—but satisfied.

[Once you found that Mitchum was not responsible for the murder, or any part of the abduction of Cheryl Claymore, you made his release top priority because no innocent person should be in custody.]

At 2:15 p.m. you take a Ramey Warrant to Judge Michaels for Kevin Bryant's arrest. You describe Bryant as 19-years-old, 5'11", 180, black hair with brown eyes. Judge Michaels signs the warrant, and you and your partner drive to Gardena to arrest Kevin Bryant.

At 7:00 p.m. Kevin's mother tells you that Kevin has not been home since Wednesday morning (May 9). She says she does not know where he went nor has she heard from him. You tell her about the arrest warrant; she indicates she will try to contact her son.

Name(s) _____   Date ____/____/____

_____

QUESTION - CHAPTER 10

1. Why did you get a Ramey Warrant for Kevin Bryant?

ARREST WARRANT
["RAMEY WARRANT"]

THE PEOPLE OF THE STATE OF CALIFORNIA,
TO ANY PEACE OFFICER: WARRANT NO.: _____

(Case number)

Proof by declaration under penalty of perjury having been made this day to me by

_____, I find that there is probable cause to believe

[Name of Officer]

                                                        [ ] MISD.

that the crime(s) of __P.C. 187/207/211/261.2__   [X] FELONY

[List Crime(s)]

were committed on or about _____4 /27 /19 _ through 4/28/_____

[List Date(s) of Offense(s)]

by the defendant named and described below.

THEREFORE, YOU ARE COMMANDED TO ARREST: __Kevin BRYANT__

[Name of Defendant(s)]

and to bring said defendant before any magistrate in L.A. County pursuant to
Penal Code Sections 821, 825, 826 and 848. In lieu of bring said defendant
before a magistrate, you may release said defendant from custody, prior to the
time limitations of Penal Code Section 825, without bail and without further
appearance before a magistrate.

Defendant is to be admitted to bail in the amount of/$/ __No Bail__

Time Issued: __2:15__ [a.m./(p.m.)]   _____

[Signature of the Judge]

Dated: ____/ / 19____   Judge of the _____Court

[MISDEMEANORS] GOOD CAUSE HAVING BEEN SHOWN by affidavit, this warrant may be
served at anytime of the day or night, as approved by my initials: _____
****

DESCRIPTION OF DEFENDANT

Sex _M_ Race _____ D.O.B. _____ Height _5'-11"_ Weight _180_

Hair _black_ Eyes _Brown_ Scars/Marks/Tattos _____

License/I.D.# _ _____ SSN _____ LAR # _____

Residence Address _____

[#/Street/City/State]

Vehicle: Year _____ Make _____ Model _____ Color _____
Info.& :
Desc. : License # _____ _____ State _____

Other Information: _____

* [The complaint underlying this warrant of arrest does not initiate a criminal]
[proceeding. See People v. Ramey (1976) 16 Cal.3d 263 and People v. Sesslin]
[(1968) 68 Cal.2d 418, 425-427, fn. 6.   ]

KCDA 4/87

COUNTY OF LOS ANGELES   **STATE OF CALIFORNIA**

<u>PROBABLE CAUSE COMPLAINT IN SUPPORT OF ARREST WARRANT</u> *
[DECLARATION IN SUPPORT OF THE "RAMEY WARRANT"]

I, _____, declare under penalty of perjury:

I am employed as a <u>Police Investigator</u> by the <u>City of Pasadena</u>.
                      [Position]   [Department]

I have probable cause to arrest <u>Kevin Bryant</u>
                                 [Name of Suspect(s)]

for the following crime(s): <u>P.C. 187/207/211/261</u>
                            [List Crimes]

[CHECK THE APPROPRIATE BOXES AND PROVIDE ATTACHMENTS]

__X__   Attached to this declaration and incorporated by reference is a written statement of facts which I have prepared. The facts set forth in this written statement are true, based upon my information and belief, except for those facts which are set forth as my own observations, which I know to be true based upon personal knowledge.

__X__   Attached to this declaration and incorporated by reference are offense reports, which are official records of the <u>Pasadena Police Department</u> I have personally reviewed each of these written reports. The facts set forth in these offense reports are true, based upon my information and belief, except for those facts which are set forth as my own observations, which I know to be true based upon personal knowledge.

_____   Incorporated in this declaration by reference is my oral affidavit to the Honorable _____ at approximately _____ [a.m./p.m.] on _____/_____/19____. This oral affidavit [in support of a search warrant] was recorded. The original tape recording will be filed with the clerk of the _____ Court.

I declare under penalty of perjury that the foregoing is true and correct.
Executed at _____, California on _____/19____

_____
[Signature of Officer]

_____
[Print or Type Name of Officer]

*[The complaint underlying this warrant of arrest does not initiate a criminal]
[proceeding. See <u>People v. Ramey</u> (1976) 16 Cal.3d 263 and <u>People v. Sesslin</u>]
[(1968) 88 Cal.2d 418, 425-427, fn. 6.   ]

Affidavit

This case involves the murder of Cheryl Claymore. On April 27, 19xx, at approximately 10:00 p.m., Ms. Claymore was abducted in Inglewood, and then taken to Pasadena where she was raped by three males. Shortly after leaving the hotel, at 4:00 a.m. on April 28th, the suspects shot Ms. Claymore five times in the head and left her for dead on Mountain Avenue near Page Place in Pasadena.

The investigation revealed that Ms. Claymore had a cellular telephone in her car which the suspects used and, after the murder, abandoned on Third Street in Inglewood. Your affiant was able to review the telephone records of the cellular telephone and discovered that the suspects made three calls between 10:00 p.m. and 11:00 p.m. on April 27th: One call was to Lisa Reece, a second to Sheryl Jones and the third to a girl in Texarcana, Texas.

Lisa Reece, a 15-year-old from Gardena, received a telephone call from Keith Rattling at 10:53 p.m. on April 27th. He told her that he was driving a "Benz" and calling her from the car telephone. Rattling also told Reece that he and his friends were taking a girl to a hotel. Ms. Reece added she heard a girl's voice in the background yell, "shut-up."

Sheryl Jones received a telephone call from Rattling on April 27th at 10:49 p.m. Rattling asked Jones if her cousin, Jamie, was home. Jones told Rattling she was not and had a short conversation with Rattling before she hung-up. Miss Jones indicated that she thought Rattling called her on a cellular telephone.

A teen-aged girl in Texarcana, Texas received a telephone call from Larounce Sands, on April 28th at about 1:00 a.m.--this would be 11:00 p.m. California time.

Your affiant obtained a search warrant for Rattling's house and served this warrant on May 9th. Rattling was arrested for murdering Ms. Claymore. Her cellular telephone and the murder weapon were recovered from his house. Rattling confessed to abducting Ms. Claymore, sexually assaulting her and being present when she was shot in her car, dumped on the street and shot twice more. Rattling named Larounce Sands and Kevin Bryant as principals to these crimes. Rattling named Sands as the shooter.

Your affiant interrogated Larounce Sands. He was already in custody at the men's county jail. Sands confessed to the crimes; his story paralleled Rattling's with the exception of who shot Ms. Claymore. Sands admitted abducting Ms. Claymore outside a liquor store in Inglewood, driving her car to pick up Kevin Bryant from his house in Gardena then driving to Pasadena where

they checked into a hotel and sexually assaulted her. Sands added
they left the hotel and drove to a small street. There, Keith
Rattling shot Ms. Claymore three times in the head, pulled her
out of the car and while she lied on the ground, shot her twice
more.

Based on the statements from Rattling and Sands it is apparent
that Kevin Bryant was part of this crime spree. Your affiant
requests a Ramey Warrant be issued in order to effect the
immediate arrest of Kevin Bryant.

May 11 (Friday)

Criminal Filings

Special Circumstances: According to the penal code, the penalty for first degree murder with special circumstances is death or life without parole (LWOP). Special circumstances is applicable in the following cases:

1. The murder was carried out for financial gain or;
2. The defendant was previously convicted of murder or;
3. The defendant has, in the current proceeding, been convicted of multiple murder or;
4. The murder was committed by an explosive device or;
5. The murder was committed while trying to avoid lawful arrest or;
6. The victim was a peace officer, federal agent or prosecutor or judge or;
7. The victim was killed while the defendant was lying in wait or;
8. The victim was killed while the defendant was engaged in committing any of the following offenses:

    (a)   Robbery
    (b)   Kidnapping
    (c)   Rape
    (d)   Sodomy
    (e)   Lewd act upon a child under 14 years old
    (f)   Oral copulation
    (g)   Burglary
    (h)   Arson, or;

9. The murder involved torture

All night Thursday, May 10, you and your partner write your investigative reports. At 10:00 a.m. you walk to the District Attorney's Office and meet Ayn Harris, Deputy District Attorney. She reviews the reports and files the following four counts against Larounce Sands and Kevin Bryant:

1. Penal Code 187(a) - Murder

2. Penal Code 207(a) - Kidnapping

3. Penal Code 264.1 - Rape

4. Penal Code 211   - Robbery

She also includes a special circumstances allegation which allows the district attorney's office to seek the death penalty and includes use of a firearm allegation during the commission of a crime.

The Juvenile District Attorney filed the same charges against Keith Rattling (with the exception of the special circumstances allegation because he's a minor). In addition, Ms. Harris will collaborate with the Juvenile Deputy District Attorney to get Keith Rattling tried as an adult.

After you file the paperwork with the court, you meet with Judge Michaels, and he signs an arrest warrant for Kevin Bryant. (See following Complaint)

Meeting With A.J.

You and your partner meet with A.J. and you tell him the news. He's happy—sincerely happy.

Mrs. Claymore prefers to meet you at the police station; she brings Wanda and Mandi. Cheryl's sister and daughter, upon hearing the news, get teary-eyed; they merely nod. For a moment, Mrs. Claymore seems taken back by the news. But only for a moment. "Now let me tell you something," she begins. "I'm no detective, but you mark my words, you have innocent people in jail. A.J. did it and now he has all that money."

You reemphasize the investigative process. She's not convinced. You tell her you'll keep her appraised of any new developments—Bryant's arrest, court dates, etc.

THE PEOPLE OF THE STATE OF CALIFORNIA,

                                   Plaintiff |

           v.

01 LAROUNCE Sands
    aka
02 KEVIN Bryant

                               Defendant(s)

Case No.

FELONY COMPLAINT
FOR ARREST WARRANT

The undersigned is informed and believes that:

COUNT 1

On or about April 28, 19xx in the County of Los Angeles, the crime of MURDER, in violation of PENAL CODE SECTION 187(a), a Felony, was committed by LAROUNCE Sands   and KEVIN Bryant   , who did willfully, unlawfully, and with malice aforethought murder Cheryl Claymore a human being.   It is further alleged that the above offense is a serious felony within the meaning of Penal Code Section 1192.7(c)(1).

It is further alleged that the murder of Cheryl Claymore was committed by defendant(s) LAROUNCE Sands   and KEVIN Bryant   while the said defendant(s) was/were engaged in the commission of the crime of robbery, within the meaning of Penal Code section 190.2(a)(17).

It is further alleged that the murder of Cheryl Claymore was committed by defendant(s) LAROUNCE Sands   and KEVIN Bryant   while the said defendant(s) was/were engaged in the commission of the crime of kidnapping, within the meaning of Penal Code section 190.2(a)(17).

It is further alleged that the murder of Cheryl Claymore was committed by defendant(s) LAROUNCE Sands   and KEVIN Bryant   while the said defendant(s) was/were engaged in the commission of the crime of rape, within the meaning of Penal Code section 190.2(a)(17).

It is further alleged that in the commission and attempted commission of the above offense a principal in said offense was armed with a firearm(s), to wit, handgun, said arming not being an element of the above offense, within the meaning of Penal Code Section 12022(a)(1).

* * * * *

COUNT 2

On or about April 28, 1991, in the County of Los Angeles, the crime of KIDNAPPING, in violation of PENAL CODE SECTION 207(a), a Felony, was committed by LAROUNCE Sands and KEVIN Bryant , who did willfully, unlawfully, forcibly and by instilling fear, steal, take, hold, detain and arrest Cheryl Claymore in Los Angeles County, California, and did take the said Cheryl Claymore into another country, state, county and another part of Los Angeles County. It is further alleged that the above offense is a serious felony within the meaning of Penal Code section 1192.7(c)(20).

It is further alleged that in the commission and attempted commission of the above offense, the defendant(s), LAROUNCE Sands , personally used a firearm within the meaning of Penal Code Section 12022.5. Said act also causing the above offense to become a serious felony within the meaning of Penal Code Section 1192.7(c)(8).

It is further alleged that in the commission and attempted commission of the above offense a principal in said offense was armed with a firearm(s), to wit, handgun, said arming not being an element of the above offense, within the meaning of Penal Code Section 12022(a)(1).

* * * * *

On or about April 28, 19xx in the County of Los Angeles, the crime of
FORCIBLE RAPE WHILE ACTING IN CONCERT, in violation of PENAL CODE SECTION
264.1, a Felony, was committed by LAROUNCE Sands   and
KEVIN Bryant   , who did willfully and unlawfully have and accomplish an act
of sexual intercourse with a person, to wit, CherylClaymore by means of force
and fear of immediate and unlawful bodily injury on said person and another
while voluntarily acting in concert with each other and another by force and
violence and against the will of Cheryl Claymore personally and by aiding and
abetting each other and another in violation of penal code sections 264.1 and
261(2).   It is further alleged that the above offense is a serious felony
within the meaning of Penal Code Section 1192.7(c)(3).

"NOTICE: Conviction of this offense will require you to register pursuant
to Penal Code Section 290. Willful failure to register is a crime."

It is further alleged that in the commission and attempted commission of
the above offense, the defendant(s), LAROUNCE Sands   and
KEVIN Bryant   personally used a firearm within the meaning of Penal Code
Section 12022.5. Said act also causing the above offense to become a serious
felony within the meaning of Penal Code Section 1192.7(c)(8).

It is further alleged that in the commission and attempted commission of
the above offense a principal in said offense was armed with a firearm(s), to
wit, handgun, said arming not being an element of the above offense, within the
meaning of Penal Code Section 12022(a)(1).

* * * * *

On or about April 28, 19xx in the County of Los Angeles, the crime of 2ND
DEGREE ROBBERY, in violation of PENAL CODE SECTION 211, a Felony, was committed
by LAROUNCE Sands   and KEVIN Bryant   who did willfully,
unlawfully, and by means of force and fear take personal property from the
person, possession, and immediate presence of Cheryl Claymore   . It is further
alleged that the above offense is a serious felony within the meaning of Penal
Code Section 1192.7(c)(19).

It is further alleged that in the commission and attempted commission of
the above offense a principal in said offense was armed with a firearm(s), to
wit, handgun, said arming not being an element of the above offense, within the
meaning of Penal Code Section 12022(a)(1).

* * * * *

Further, attached hereto and incorporated herein are official reports and
documents of a law enforcement agency which the undersigned believes establish
probable cause for the arrest of defendant(s) LAROUNCE Sands   and
KEVIN Bryant   , for the above-listed crimes. Wherefore, a warrant of arrest
is requested for KEVIN Bryant

I DECLARE UNDER PENALTY OF PERJURY THAT THE FOREGOING IS TRUE AND CORRECT AND THAT THIS COMPLAINT, CASE NUMBER xxxxxxx , CONSISTS OF 4 COUNT(S).

Executed at Pasadena, County of Los Angeles, on May 14, 19xx

_____

DECLARANT AND COMPLAINANT

· ·

DISTRICT ATTORNEY

BY: _____

AGENCY: PASA INV. DETS   I/O: ID NO: PHONE NO:
DR NO: OPERATOR: vf PRELIM.TIME EST.: 1 Hrs.

DEFENDANT	CII NO.	DOB	BOOKING NO.	BAIL RECOM'D	CUSTODY R'TN DATE
Larounce Sands				NO BAIL	
Kevin Bryant				NO BAIL	

It appearing to the Court that probable cause exists for the issuance of a warrant of arrest for the above named defendant(s), the warrant is so ordered.

_____
Judge of the above entitled Court

FELONY COMPLAINT - ORDER HOLDING TO ANSWER - P.C. SECTION 872

It appearing to me from the evidence presented that the following offense(s) has/have been committed and that there is sufficient cause to believe that the following defendant(s) guilty thereof, to wit:

(Strike out or add as applicable)

LAROUNCE Sands

Count No.	Charge	Charge Range	Special Allegation	Alleg. Effect
1	PC187(a)	Check Code	PC190.2(a)(17)	LWOP/Death
			PC190.2(a)(17)	LWOP/Death
			PC190.2(a)(17)	LWOP/Death
			PC12022(a)(1)	+1 YR
2	PC207(a)	3-5-8	PC12022.5(a)	3-4-5
			PC12022(a)(1)	+1 YR
3	PC264.1	5-7-9	PC12022.5(a)	3-4-5
			PC12022(a)(1)	+1 YR
4	PC211	2-3-5	PC12022(a)(1)	+1 YR

KEVIN Bryant

Count No.	Charge	Charge Range	Special Allegation	Alleg. Effect
1	PC187(a)	Check Code	PC190.2(a)(17)	LWOP/Death
			PC190.2(a)(17)	LWOP/Death
			PC190.2(a)(17)	LWOP/Death
			PC12022(a)(1)	+1 YR
2	PC207(a)	3-5-8	PC12022(a)(1)	+1 YR
3	PC264.1	5-7-9	PC12022.5(a)	3-4-5
			PC12022(a)(1)	+1 YR
4	PC211	2-3-5	PC12022(a)(1)	+1 YR

I order that defendant(s) be held to answer therefor and be admitted to bail in the sum of:

LAROUNCE Sands _____ Dollars

KEVIN Bryant _____ Dollars

Name(s) _____   Date _____/_____/_____

_____

QUESTIONS - CHAPTER 10 CONTINUED

2. Is the investigation over? Why? Why not?

3. What do you do now?

   A. Concentrate solely on arresting Kevin Bryant? Explain.

   B. Let the District Attorney's personnel handle the case now? Explain.

   C. Get blood and saliva samples from Rattling and Sands for DNA testing? Explain.

May 12 (Saturday)

Investigation Continues

The pressure of solving the case is now over, but you still have work to do.

You and your partner drive to Gardena and meet Mr. Sands, Larounce's father. You inspect Larounce's El Camino for evidence. No blood, hair or other possible evidence can be found. After you take photographs, you leave the car with Mr. Sands.

On May 16 (Wednesday) you and your partner drive to the juvenile detention facility to get blood and saliva samples from Keith Rattling subsequent to a search warrant issued by Judge Daniels. In your presence, the nurse draws blood and gets a saliva sample from Rattling. You take the evidence immediately to the Sheriff's Crime Lab.

On May 21 (Monday) you call Kary Short, who received three calls from Ms. Claymore's cellular telephone on the night after the murder. Ms. Short has a baby by Larounce Sands. She remembers that several weeks back Larounce called her from a cellular telephone, and he said he was driving on the freeway. She also tells you that Kevin Bryant and Keith Rattling are close friends of hers.

Later that day, by order of Judge Michaels, you and your partner drive to county jail and serve a search warrant on Sands to obtain blood and saliva samples. These evidence samples are immediately taken to the crime lab (See following search warrant).

SEARCH WARRANT AND AFFIDAVIT
(AFFIDAVIT)

_____ _____ _____ , being sworn, says that on the basis of the information contained within
(Name of Affiant)
this Search Warrant and Affidavit and the attached and incorporated **Statement of Probable Cause,** he/she has probable
cause to believe and does believe that the property described below is lawfully seizable pursuant to Penal Code Section 1524,
as indicated below, and is now located at the locations set forth below. Wherefore, affiant requests that this Search Warrant be
issued.

_____ _____ , NIGHT SEARCH REQUESTED: YES [   ] NO [·X·x]
(Signature of Affiant)

(SEARCH WARRANT)

THE PEOPLE OF THE STATE OF CALIFORNIA TO ANY SHERIFF, POLICEMAN OR PEACE OFFICER IN THE COUNTY

OF LOS ANGELES: proof by affidavit having been made before me by _____ . _____
(Name of Affiant)
that there is probable cause to believe that the property described herein may be found at the locations set forth herein and that it
is lawfully seizable pursuant to Penal Code Section 1524 as indicated below by "x" (s) in that it:

_____ was stolen or embezzled

___xx___ was used as the means of committing a felony

_____ is possessed by a person with the intent to use it as means of committing a public offense or is possessed by another to whom he or she may have
delivered it for the purpose of concealing it or preventing its discovery,

___xx___ tends to show that a felony has been committed or that a particular person has committed a felony,

_____ tends to show that sexual exploitation of a child, in violation of P.C. Section 311.3, has occurred or is occurring;

YOU ARE THEREFORE COMMANDED TO SEARCH:

Keith Rattling, 17 years old, DOB of xx/xx/19xx, 5'9", 175lbs, black hair, brown eyes
Resides at xxxx xxxxxxxx xx Gardena, CA

FOR THE FOLLOWING PROPERTY:

Blood and saliva samples for DNA screening

AND TO SEIZE IT IF FOUND and bring it forthwith before me, or this court, at the courthouse of this court. This Search Warrant
and incorporated Affidavit was sworn to and subscribed before me this _____ day of _____ , 19 ___ ,
at _____ A.M./P.M. Wherefore, I find probable cause for the issuance of this Search Warrant and do issue it.

_____ , NIGHT SEARCH APPROVED: YES [   ] NO [   ]
(Signature of Magistrate)

Judge of the **Superior/Municipal** Court, _____ Judicial District

DA-1506-A—78S346W3—8/86   SW & A1

Your Affiant has been a police officer for over nine years, and during this time he has participated in the investigation of several violent crimes including murders. I have been assigned to the Detective Section, Crimes Against Persons Unit, of the Pasadena Police Department since February, 19xx. I have investigated numerous violent crimes (homicides, attempted homicides, assaults and robberies) and have received formal training in these areas. Your Affiant received formal training in homicide investigations through the Los Angeles Sheriff's Academy and the California District Attorney's Homicide Symposium.

On April 28, 19xx at approximately 6:00 a.m., your Affiant was called to the Pasadena area of Page Place and Mountain Avenue to investigate a murder. Upon my arrival, I observed the dead body of a female in the middle of the street. The victim had been shot several times in the head with small caliber bullets. The victim was identified as Cheryl Claymore from Hawthorne.

The investigation has revealed that on April 27, 19xx at approximately 10:00 p.m., Ms. Claymore left the residence of Rochelle Moren, of Inglewood, and drove to a nearby liquor store to buy snacks for her daughter. Ms. Claymore never returned to Ms. Moren's home.

The investigation further revealed that Cheryl Claymore had been abducted outside the liquor store by two males, then taken to two hotels, one being the Mercury Hotel in Pasadena, in the course of about five hours. At these hotels, Ms. Claymore was raped by the males. A third male joined the group after these suspects left the first hotel. Cellular telephone records from Ms. Claymore's car revealed that Keith Rattling had made two calls from this phone during the hours Cheryl Claymore was abducted. Rattling told a female friend, Lisa Reece, that he was with his "homeboys," they had a girl and they were taking her to a hotel. Rattling was arrested. Subsequently, Cheryl's cellular telephone was found in his bedroom.

Keith Rattling admitted that he was part of Claymore's abduction. He also admitted having sexual intercourse with Cheryl, "I had sex with her, but she wanted it."

Certain body fluids, including seminal fluid, were discovered on a menstrual pad that Cheryl Claymore wore during her abduction. It is the opinion of your Affiant that seminal fluid from Keith Rattling will be found on this piece of evidence. Your Affiant requests that blood be drawn from Keith Rattling and a saliva sample be taken in order to conduct DNA analysis.

Name(s) _____   Date _____/_____/_____

_____

QUESTIONS - CHAPTER 10 CONTINUED

4. Why are you getting blood and saliva samples?

5. How will the above help you in your investigation?

6. Why did you get a search warrant in order to collect the samples?

May 22 (Tuesday)

The Town Hotel

A.J. Claymore calls you and says he has Cheryl's credit card statement; it shows two charges for hotels on the dates of April 27 and April 28: the Mercury Hotel, in Pasadena, and the Town Hotel, in Alhambra.

You contact Mr. Richards, the Town Hotel manager, who was working the evening of April 27, and show him a picture of Cheryl. Even though Cheryl was murdered two months ago, Mr. Richards remembers her and tells you she wore her hair in a style different from that of the picture. He is correct. He tells you the girl and a male requested a room. He adds that they were both calm. She paid with a credit card and produced identification. He shows you the registration card. It has the following written information:

NAME: Trevenon Sands
STREET: 211 137th
CITY: Comptona [sic] STATE: CA
CAR LICENSE: A350279 STATE: CA
MAKE OF CAR: Bentz [sic] NUMBER OF PERSONS: 2

Actual registration for room paid by Cheryl Claymore—The Town Hotel

Mr. Richards describes the male as 23 to 24 years of age, 5'8" with black hair.

You show Mr. Richards two photo lineups, one with Larounce Sands' picture among the six photographs. The other lineup has Keith Rattling's picture. Mr. Richards cannot identify either male.

May 23 (Wednesday)

Evidence Against Larounce Sands

At 11:00 a.m. you drive to the Los Angeles County Jail and ask the deputies to take Larounce Sands' fingerprints. By order of Judge Michaels, from a motion by the Deputy District Attorney Harris, you have Sands fill out a handwriting exemplar. The writing appears similar to the writing on the hotel registration slip. You take the fingerprints to your department's fingerprint expert, then you take the writing exemplar to the Los Angeles Sheriff's Crime Lab.

Police Screw-up

Later, on this same day, A.J. Claymore shows up at the station with a .25 caliber shell casing. He tells you that he found the casing in the back seat of Cheryl's Mercedes Benz wedged between the seat cushions. (Guess what? You and other law enforcement personnel are not infallible.)

May 24 (Thursday)

Photo lineups for Suei Lee

You get a picture of Kevin Bryant and put together a photo lineup. This photo lineup along with two other lineups with pictures of Keith Rattling and Larounce Sands are taken to Suei Lee. She looks at Kevin Bryant's picture, points to it, and says, "This guy looks very close to the guy with the girl." Suei says, "He's the one that requested the second room." She looks at the other two lineups but can't identify anyone.

May, June and July

Analyzed Evidence

Firearms

Deputy Shear, of the Firearms Identification Section of the Los Angeles County Sheriff's Crime Lab, examined the bullets found in Cheryl's body at the crime scene, as well as the casings found at the crime scene and in the car. He concluded that the bullets and casings were fired from the recovered .25 caliber Raven semi-automatic pistol. The gun was also analyzed by serology criminalists because there was blood on the slide (upper portion of the gun that slides to eject the casings and chamber the bullets into proper position for firing). This blood was the same type as Cheryl Claymore's blood.

Fingerprints

The latent fingerprints found on Cheryl Claymore's car were a match to the following two suspects:

Keith Rattling was identified as the person whose fingerprints were found on the exterior driver's door.

Larounce Sands was identified as the person whose fingerprint was found on the exterior right rear passenger door window. He was identified as the person whose right palm print was found on the exterior left rear passenger door from the Mercedes Benz.

Documents

The document examiner from the Los Angeles County Sheriff's Crime Lab identified Larounce Sands as the person who wrote on the registration slip of the Town Hotel.

DNA

The semen found on Ms. Claymore's panties had a DNA banding pattern originating from at least three individuals. One DNA banding pattern obtained from the panties matched the DNA banding pattern obtained from the blood swatch of Larounce Sands. A second DNA banding pattern was obtained from the panties; the source has not been identified. The third banding pattern from the panties matched the DNA banding pattern from the blood swatch of Keith Rattling. The statistical frequency for these identifications is 1 in 2.1 billion.

LOS ANGELES COUNTY SHERIFF'S DEPARTMENT

SCIENTIFIC SERVICES BUREAU

FIREARMS IDENTIFICATION SECTION

REC'D FROM Det. - Pasadena P.D.	FILE
DATE 05-08-1991	**RECEIPT**
CAL. .25 auto	**MAKE** Raven Arms
MODEL MP - 25	**TYPE** Semi auto pistol
SERIAL NO.	**LOCATION** Backstrap of pistol

COUNTRY U.S.A.	CARTRIDGE CAPACITY 1 + 6	BARREL LENGTH 2 3/8"	FINISH Nickel

ADDITIONAL INFO - CONDITION - OTHER MARKS - BROKEN/MISSING PARTS

S - Rattling, Keith   C-187 P.C.

V - Claymore, Cheryl

S/A TRIGGER PULL 7 1/2 Lbs.	IS THIS NORMAL Yes	D/A TRIGGER PULL ---	IS THIS NORMAL ---	FIRED SINCE LAST CLEANING Yes
NO. TIMES TEST FIRED 2	DID FIREARM FUNCTION NORMALLY DURING TEST FIRING - IF NO, EXPLAIN Yes			

GRC	CALIBER .25 auto	NO. L&G 6	TWIST L	LAND IMP. WIDTH .050	GROOVE IMP. WIDTH .076

OTHER EVIDENCE WITH FIREARM - OPINIONS - COMMENTS

- See page #2 for other evidence -

FIREARMS EXAMINER	SIGNATURE
EMP. NO	DATE COMPLETED

REPORT CONTINUATION

OTHER EVIDENCE:

Item #1 - One Coroner's envelope (case #   ) containing one
expended .25 caliber FMJ bullet, Wt. = 50.1 GRS.

Item #2 - One Coroner's envelope (case #   ) containing one
expended .25 caliber FMJ bullet, Wt. = 50.2 GRS.

Item #3 - One Coroner's envelope (case #   ) containing one
expended .25 caliber FMJ bullet, Wt. = 50.1 GRS.

Item #4 - One Coroner's envelope (case #   ) containing one
expended .25 caliber FMJ bullet (fragmented)
Wt. = 46.7 GRS.

Item #5 - One envelope containing one expended .25 caliber FMJ
bullet, Wt. = 50.1 GRS.

Item #6 - One envelope containing one expended .25 auto caliber
cartridge case (Win)

Item #7 - One envelope containing one expended .25 auto caliber
cartridge case (Win)

Item #8 - One envelope containing one expended .25 auto caliber
cartridge case (Win)

Examination of the evidence submitted in this case revealed the
following:

1. The expended .25 caliber bullets contained in items #1,
    #2, #3, #5 and the expended cartridge cases contained in
    items #6, #7, & #8 were positively fired in the Raven
    pistol described on page #1 of this report.

2. The examination of the .25 caliber bullet contained in
    item #4 was inconclusive due to excessive mutilation.

CHEMICAL PROCESSING EXAMINATION REPORT
Scientific Services Bureau
Identification Section
Chemical Processing Unit
2020 West Beverly Blvd.
Los Angeles, California 90057

Agency: Pasadena Police   File Number:
Investigator: Receipt Number:
Charge: 187 P. C., Murder   Coroner's Case Number:
Victim: Claymore Cheryl   Date Received:
Suspect:Rattling, Keith   Report Date:

Evidence Submitted:

   One Raven 25 auto handgun, serial #
   One magazine

Results:

   The above items were processed for latent prints. No prints obtained

Disposition of evidence:

        All evidence forwarded to Scientific Services Bureau -
        Firearms section on

        By: _____

            Forensic Identification Specialist
            Identification Section

Assigned To: Homicide Bureau

City of Pasadena

207 NORTH GARFIELD AVENUE
PASADENA, CALIFORNIA 91101

POLICE DEPARTMENT

Investigative Division
Detective Section
Fingerprint Unit

CASE #_____

IDENTIFICATION COMPARISON CERTIFICATION

I, _____ , a Fingerprint Technician,
having qualified as an Expert Fingerprint Identification
Witness, have examined the prints(s) appearing on the
attached exemplar bearing the name of LAROUNCE Sands
and having made a comparison with the following:

LATENT LIFT FROM EXTERIOR SIDE OF PASSENGER DOOR GLASS

_____

_____

_____

_____

_____

I am prepared to testify in court that the prints appearing
on the aforementioned exhibits were made by, and are the
prints of the same person. This identification has been
verified by Los Angeles County Deputy Sheriff, _____
_____, a qualified Expert Fingerprint
Identification Witness.

SIGNATURE_____ DATE _____

ATTACHMENT

City of Pasadena

207 NORTH GARFIELD AVENUE
PASADENA, CALIFORNIA 91101

POLICE DEPARTMENT

Investigative Division
Detective Section
Fingerprint Unit

CASE #_____

IDENTIFICATION COMPARISON CERTIFICATION

I, _____, a Fingerprint Technician,
having qualified as an Expert Fingerprint Identification
Witness, have examined the prints(s) appearing on the
attached exemplar bearing the name of _LAROUNCE Sands_____
and having made a comparison with the following:

LATENT LIFT FROM EXTERIOR OF PASSENGER SIDE OF VEHICLE
_____

_____

_____

_____

_____

_____

_____

I am prepared to testify in court that the prints appearing
on the aforementioned exhibits were made by, and are the
prints of the same person. This identification has been
verified by Los Angeles County Deputy Sheriff, _____
_____, a qualified Expert Fingerprint
Identification Witness.

SIGNATURE_____ DATE _____

ATTACHMENT

City of Pasadena

207 NORTH GARFIELD AVENUE
PASADENA, CALIFORNIA 91101

POLICE DEPARTMENT

Investigative Division
Detective Section
Fingerprint Unit

CASE #_____

IDENTIFICATION COMPARISON CERTIFICATION

I, _____, a Fingerprint Technician,
having qualified as an Expert Fingerprint Identification
Witness, have examined the prints(s) appearing on the
attached exemplar bearing the name of <u>KEITH Rattling</u>
and having made a comparison with the following:

_____ (3) LATENT LIFTS FROM EXTERIOR DRIVERS DOOR _____

_____

_____

_____

_____

_____

_____

I am prepared to testify in court that the prints appearing
on the aforementioned exhibits were made by, and are the
prints of the same person. This identification has been
verified by Los Angeles County Deputy Sheriff, _____
_____, a qualified Expert Fingerprint
Identification Witness.

SIGNATURE_____ DATE _____

ATTACHMENT

**LOS ANGELES COUNTY
SHERRIFF'S DEPARTMENT**

Suspect: Sands , LAROUNCE
Victim: ---
Agency: PASADENA P.D.
Investigator:
File No:
Charge: 187 DC
Receipt No:
Date:

Page 1 of 1

SCIENTIFIC SERVICES BUREAU
Questioned Documents Section
2020 W. Beverly Boulevard
Los Angeles, California 90057

D O C U M E N T   E X A M I N A T I O N   R E P O R T

QUESTIONED DOCUMENTS:

1 -   Town   motel receipt number

EXEMPLARS:

1 -   Fingerprint card

1 -   Handwriting Exemplar

OPINION:

The questioned printing is by the writer on the exemplars.

DOCUMENT EXAMINER

REPORT OF LABORATORY EXAMINATION

CELLMARK
D I A G N O S T I C S

Cellmark Diagnostics

20271 Goldenrod Lane
Germantown, Maryland 20874

Telephone

Supervising Criminalist
Los Angeles County Sheriff's Department
Scientific Services Bureau
2020 West Beverly Boulevard
Los Angeles, CA 90057

Re: Your Case No.
     Cellmark Case No.

EXHIBITS:

The following items were received for analysis on

ID#	DESCRIPTION
1	Three swabs labelled "...vaginal sample..."
3	1.25 swabs labelled "...rectal sample..."
4	One swab labelled "...external genital sample..."
5	Pieces of gauze and cotton labelled "...menstrual pad"
6	Black cloth cuttings labelled "...Black panties..."
7	Black nylon material cuttings labelled "...nylons..."
8	One blood swatch labelled "Claymore Cheryl"
9	One blood swatch labelled "Rattling Keith"
10	One blood swatch labelled "Larounce Sands "

RESULTS:

DNA was extracted from the items listed above. DNA banding patterns were obtained from the vaginal swabs (item 1), the rectal sample (item 3), the menstrual pad (item 5), the black panties (item 6), the black nylons (item 7), the blood swatch labelled Cheryl Claymore (item 8), the blood swatch labelled Keith Rattling (item 9), and the blood swatch labelled Larounce Sands   (item 10) using the restriction enzyme HinfI and the four single-locus probes MS1(D1S7), MS31(D7S21), MS43 (D12S11), and g3(D7S22).

An insufficient quantity of high molecular weight DNA was obtained from the genital swab (item 4) to continue testing.

A DNA banding pattern originating from at least four individuals was obtained from the vaginal swabs. One DNA banding pattern obtained from the vaginal swabs matches the DNA banding pattern obtained from the blood swatch labelled CherylClaymore. A second DNA banding pattern obtained from the vaginal swabs matches the DNA banding pattern obtained from the blood swatch labelled Keith Rattling. A third DNA banding pattern obtained from the vaginal swabs contains six bands which are similar to six of the seven bands in the DNA banding pattern obtained from the blood swatch

Report for Case No.

Page Two

labelled Larounce Sands . A fourth DNA banding pattern was obtained from the vaginal swabs whose source has not been determined.

The DNA banding patterns obtained from the black nylons matches the DNA banding pattern obtained from the blood swatch labelled Cheryl Claymore. No other DNA banding patterns were obtained from the black nylons.

The DNA banding pattern obtained from the rectal sample is similar to the DNA banding pattern obtained from the blood swatch labelled Cheryl Claymore. No other DNA banding patterns were obtained from the rectal sample.

The DNA banding pattern obtained from the menstrual pad originated from at least four individuals. One DNA banding pattern obtained from the menstrual pad matches the DNA banding pattern obtained from the blood swatch labelled Larounce Sands . A second DNA banding pattern obtained from the menstrual pad contains six bands which are similar to six of the eight bands obtained from the blood swatch labelled KeithRattling. A third DNA banding pattern obtained from the menstrual pad contains three bands which are similar to three of the seven bands obtained from the blood swatch labelled Cheryl Claymore. A fourth DNA banding pattern was obtained from the menstrual pad whose source has not been determined.

A DNA banding pattern originating from at least three individuals was obtained from the panties. One DNA banding pattern obtained from the panties matches the DNA banding pattern obtained from the blood swatch labelled Larounce Sands . A second DNA banding pattern was obtained from the panties whose source has not been determined. One additional band obtained from the panties matches one of the eight bands in the DNA banding pattern obtained from the blood swatch labelled Keith Rattling.

The DNA banding patterns obtained from the vaginal swabs, the menstrual pad and the panties whose sources have not been determined are all similar to each other.

CONCLUSION:

No conclusion can be reached concerning the genital swab.

No conclusion can be reached concerning the band in the panties which matched one band observed in the DNA banding pattern obtained from the blood of Keith Rattling.

The DNA banding pattern obtained from the rectal sample was similar to the DNA banding pattern obtained from the blood swatch labelled Cheryl Claymore.

The DNA banding pattern obtained from the nylons matched the DNA banding pattern obtained from the blood swatch labelled Cheryl Claymore.

Similarity was observed between the third DNA banding pattern obtained from the vaginal swabs and the DNA banding pattern obtained from the blood swatch labelled Larounce Sands . Larounce Sands cannot be identified or excluded as a source of the DNA obtained from the vaginal swabs.

Similarity was observed between the DNA banding pattern obtained from the menstrual pad and the DNA banding pattern obtained from the blood swatch labelled Keith Rattling. Keith Rattling cannot be identified or excluded as the source of the DNA obtained from the menstrual pad.

Using four single-locus probes sequentially (MS1, MS31, MS43, and g3), the approximate frequencies in the Black, Caucasian, and Western Hispanic populations of the DNA banding pattern obtained from the vaginal swabs and the blood swatch labelled Keith Rattling are as follows:

Population data base	Frequency
	1 in 490 million
	1 in 400 billion
	1 in 30 billion

Using four single-locus probes sequentially (MS1, MS31, MS43, and g3), the approximate frequencies in the Black, Caucasian, and Western Hispanic populations of the DNA banding pattern obtained from the panties, the menstrual pad and the blood swatch labelled Larounce Sands are as follows:

Population data base	Frequency
	1 in 2.1 billion
	1 in 22 billion
	1 in 7.7 billion

_____   _____

Population Geneticist   Staff Molecular Biologist

Tire Marks and Shoe Print

The following items could not be matched:

1. Tire marks at the scene to Cheryl's Benz

2. Shoe print—pattern not recognizable enough

Miscellaneous Items

The following items were fingerprinted but no match could be made because of the print's quality or because no prints were found:

1. Cassette tapes - found at the murder scene

2. *Zig-Zag* papers - found on the street near the purse

3. Makeup items - found in the purse at the murder scene

4. Cup - found at the Mercury Hotel

5. Papers - found in the purse or scattered in the parking lot

6. Papers - found in the Mercedes Benz

Blood

The following items were tested for human blood but no match was made:

1. Red stains on Joe Mitchum's gloves

2. Red stains on Keith Rattling's pants

You make no further follow-up from the list provided by the Mercury Hotel of those people who spent the night on April 27 but left prior to your arrival.

No testing was done to identify the alcoholic beverage in the cup at the Mercury Hotel.

One Year Later

Investigation Regarding Kevin Bryant

You and your partner have consistently checked N.C.I.C. this past year to see if Kevin Bryant may have been arrested on the murder warrant.

During this time, you get a telephone call from the Virginia State Police. They tell you that they have arrested a man with an alias of Kevin Bryant and with the same birth date of the person responsible for Cheryl Claymore's death. They send you this person's fingerprints; he is not the Kevin Bryant from Gardena.

Also, during this time period, you have talked with a recreation employee at Rollins Park, (the park where Keith Rattling said they picked up Bryant) who tells you that he recently saw Bryant in the Gardena area. You ask this person to call the police if he sees Kevin Bryant again.

Name(s) _____   Date ____/____/____

_____

QUESTIONS - CHAPTER 10 CONTINUED

7. Are you surprised to find two credit card charges for two hotels on April 27 and April 28? Why? Why not?

8. Why is the registration slip at the Town Hotel important?

9. Why did you get a new set of fingerprints from Larounce Sands?

10. Why do you have Sands fill out a handwriting exemplar?

Name(s) _____   Date ____/____/____

_____

QUESTIONS - CHAPTER 10 CONTINUED

11. What is the significance of A.J. finding a shell casing in Cheryl's car? What problems may arise in court because of this?

12. What is your feeling about Suei Lee's identification of Kevin Bryant in the photo lineup?

13. What did the firearms analysis reveal?

14. What did the fingerprint analysis reveal?

Name(s) _____   Date ____ / ____ / ____

_____

QUESTIONS - CHAPTER 10 CONTINUED

15. What did the document analysis reveal?

16. What did the DNA analysis reveal?

17. You did not test the beverage found in the cup at the Mercury Hotel. Why?

May 1 (Friday)—A Year Later

Locating Kevin Bryant

At 1:45 p.m. Detective Massip of the Torrance Police Department calls you and says they have arrested Kevin Bryant. He tells you Kevin Bryant, using the name Terry Calloway, was arrested on April 30 for an attempted bank robbery. He walked into a Bank of America and handed a teller a note demanding money.

Luckily, a police officer walked into the bank to conduct personal business. When the teller saw the officer, she yelled, "The police are here." Bryant panicked, ran out of the bank and was arrested after a foot pursuit. (Bryant tore up the note while he was running and tossed it, but it was a *very* short pursuit, and the officer was able to collect most of the pieces and tape them back together.) FBI Agents handled the follow-up investigation. They read Bryant his *Miranda* Rights and tried to interview Bryant regarding the attempted robbery, but he requested an attorney.

Name(s) _____   Date ____/____/____

_____

QUESTION - CHAPTER 10 CONTINUED

18. What is the impact of Bryant's request for an attorney?

May 1 (Friday)

Interview With Torrance Police Officers

You drive to Torrance Police Department and interview Detective Massip, Reserve Officer Elkins and Paramedic Pagliano.

Detective Massip tells you Bryant complained of a respiratory problem and wanted to be transferred to Los Angeles County Jail. Massip says that Bryant is at a local hospital and that he and another detective will be taking him to county jail. You request that they return Bryant to Torrance so you can take custody of him. Massip agrees.

Massip adds that he heard Bryant talking to Paramedic Pagliano about a murder as he was getting into the ambulance. He's not sure exactly what Bryant said about the murder, so he suggests you call Pagliano.

You call the fire station and speak with Paramedic Pagliano. He tells you that he had a general conversation with Bryant about school and athletics before he asked about the murder warrant. Bryant said, "I'll beat the charge." He went on to tell Pagliano that last year he got a "head job" from a girl picked up by his "homeboys," Larounce and Keith. Bryant added that Keith is crazy, so crazy that he shot the girl in the head. He said he didn't actually see Keith shoot her because his "homies" took him home so he could watch a Raiders football game. He just heard about it the next day.

They return Bryant and put him in a holding cell. You interview Reserve Officer Elkins. Elkins tells you he was assigned to watch Bryant at the hospital. Elkins adds that he didn't know anything about the murder charge until Bryant started talking about the murder. He said he kept silent while Bryant bragged about his "homies" and about "some girl" that was in "this Benz" when they picked him up at his house. He said they drove around a while and eventually went to an apartment where he and the girl talked. He liked the girl, but he worried about her knowing his address. But now it doesn't matter because when they all got into the car again Larounce said, "F_ _k this" and shot her twice.

Name(s) _____   Date _____ / _____ / _____

_____

CHAPTER 10 QUESTIONS CONTINUED

19. Why did you want Bryant taken from the hospital to the Torrance Police Department?

20. What, if any, statements did Bryant make to Paramedic Pagliano and Officer Elkins that were incriminating?

21. Can you believe Bryant? Why? Why not?

May 1 (Friday)

Kevin Bryant's Interrogation

Principal: According to the penal code, principals are persons who commit a crime, or aid and abet in its commission, or if not present have advised or encouraged its commission.

Accessory: The penal code defines an accessory as one who, after a felony has been committed, conceals or aids a principal in such a felony with the intent to help the principal avoid or escape arrest, trial, conviction or punishment. The accessory must have knowledge that the principal has committed such a felony or has been charged with the crime.

Before returning to the police station, you drive Bryant to the murder scene and sit silently for a few minutes. Bryant, who has been talkative throughout the drive, doesn't say a word. At 6:00 p.m. at the Pasadena Police Station, the taped interrogation begins. You read Bryant his *Miranda* Rights; he says he understands them and is willing to talk to you without an attorney.

Bryant identifies Keith Rattling, Larounce Sands and Cheryl Claymore from photographs you lay in front of him. He tells you that one evening a year ago Sands called him and said he had some drinks and "bud" (marijuana). He says Sands, Rattling and the girl came to his house in her Benz. They cruised, smoked, drank and tried to find *some* hotel that Sands had a key to. He adds the girl offered to get a room at another hotel, and they ended up at the Mercury Hotel. Bryant says he and the girl registered for two rooms. In one of the rooms he conversed with her and felt her breasts. He denied any sexual contact but said Sands and Rattling had some.

Bryant further explains that while he was alone with the girl, she told him she was scared of Sands and Rattling and that they had forced her to be with them. She told him she was married and needed to be home by 2:00 or 3:00 a.m. Bryant tells you he got angry with Sands and Rattling because he didn't know they had abducted the girl. He tells you that when they checked out and were walking to the car, Sands and Rattling lagged behind and were whispering. On the way home, they stopped the car and Sands said, "F__k this" and shot the girl. Kevin Bryant explains that he was the front passenger when Keith drove the car away from the hotel. Larounce was behind him and the girl was behind Keith. Kevin tells you, however, that on the way back to Gardena, it was Keith who kept asking Larounce where he was going. Kevin adds Larounce was so drunk he forgot he left his car in Inglewood.

You explain DNA to Bryant. He knows where you're coming from and confesses that he and the girl did have sexual contact. But, he says, the girl undressed for him. He masturbated and ejaculated on her vagina; he never penetrated her.

Bryant asks, "Am I an accessory to murder?"

Name(s) _____   Date ____/____/____

_____

QUESTIONS - CHAPTER 10 CONTINUED

22. You knew that Bryant had requested to talk to an attorney when he was in custody with the FBI, yet you interrogated him. Why?

23. Is Bryant an accessory to murder? Explain.

24. Who do you think shot Cheryl Claymore? Explain.

Name(s) _____   Date _____/_____/_____

_____

QUESTIONS - CHAPTER 10 CONTINUED

25. What do you do next?

    A. Nothing, your investigation is over? Explain.

    B. Interview Bryant again? Explain.

    C. Obtain blood and saliva samples from Bryant for DNA testing? Explain.

May 5 (Tuesday)

Deputy District Attorney, Ayn Harris, requests that Judge Michaels order that Kevin Bryant provide a blood and saliva sample for DNA analysis. On May 7 you drive to Los Angeles County Jail and witness a nurse take a blood and saliva sample from Bryant. You take these samples to the Los Angeles County Sheriff's Crime Lab.

Four months later, on September 3, you are told the DNA results of Kevin Bryant: DNA analysis concluded that Kevin Bryant was a donor of semen found on Cheryl's panties. Bryant claims, and may continue to claim in court, that his semen could not have entered Cheryl, but this is moot. His semen puts him at the crime scene and provides proof that he is a principal to the abduction, rape, robbery and murder of the victim whose body was found in the early morning hours on April 27 on Mountain Avenue in Pasadena.

You have continued to keep Cheryl Claymore's family updated. Now, you can advise them that Larounce Sands, Keith Rattling and Kevin Bryant, the persons responsible for the murder of Cheryl, are now *all* in custody.

Congratulations, you have finished your investigation!

CPSIA information can be obtained
at www.ICGtesting.com
Printed in the USA
FFOW01n0250090118
44435585-44198FF